NATTITUDE

# NATTITUDE

NATALIE HAHN COXE

Palmetto Publishing Group
Charleston, SC

*Nattitude*
Copyright © 2020 by Natalie Hahn Coxe
All rights reserved

First Edition

Printed in the United States

ISBN-13: 978-1-64111-746-3
ISBN-10: 1-64111-746-X

*To Ragland, Baxter, and my parents for being my reason why.*

*To the Florentines who remind me of the gift of growing up in a small town and for showing my family strength and love.*

*To my girls who have been, and always will be, eight of my greatest blessings.*

*To Hattie and Sumter. This shouldn't come as a surprise.*

# CHAPTER 1
# NATTITUDE

Nattitude: A tough, go-get-'em, fast-paced, "doesn't take anything from anyone" attitude. A term used to describe the attitude that I would need to get through cancer. The cool thing was, this is the attitude I have always had. Since birth, actually. My parents enjoy reminiscing about my birth story. I made my debut on my own time and early, to be exact. So early that the doctor who was scheduled to deliver me was not around, so they grabbed a doctor from the hall and pulled him to the foot of the bed. Moments later, I was born.

My dad said he watched me take in my first few minutes on this earth in the hospital bassinet. I looked around the room, and he told my mother,

"She looks bored." Throughout my childhood, I hated waiting. I have a clear visual of me as a four-year-old pushing a little girl into the pool while we were standing in line for swim lessons because she was too afraid to jump to the lifeguard in the three-foot-deep pool. Move it along, sister! Patience has never been a virtue of mine. I've tried to work on breathing and taking a moment, but the truth is, it just ain't for me.

For years, my parents would try and slow me down. I would eat fast, talk fast, and walk fast. Family ski trips for me were always an opportunity to race down the ski lift that took me to the top of the mountain, leaving my parents and brother behind. I gained no greater joy than finishing first, and it didn't matter the sport or activity. But as I grew older, I began to slow my pace just a bit. I began to enjoy going with the flow of traffic more than I used to, and I found that time was much more precious than I realized as a child.

I often tried to change the way that I viewed life and the obstacles that I encountered, but as fate would have it, I knew that the personality I had always embodied was just...Nattitude. The God-given Nattitude that I had was so much more than just the personality of a feisty, little girl. It was the spirit of a fighter.

## CHAPTER 2
# TODAY

There was no history of ovarian cancer in my family. "A freak occurrence," as many would say. Stage 3C dysgerminoma: A type of ovarian cancer that affects very few women each year. It is estimated that there will be 239,000 new cases of ovarian cancer each year worldwide. Of that, 152,000 women will die from the disease. Grave statistics. Try finding that on WebMD after being smacked in the face with a cancer diagnosis as a teenager.

The familiarity of it all each time I head back to the doctor for my annual checkup still stings. Not a day passes that I don't recall this chapter of my life. It has now been seven years of remembering and counting. It'll never end, I'm sure of that.

There's no respite for ovarian cancer. Once it's a part of your life, it will always be. You just learn to live with the new label: the girl with cancer.

My vision for this book is to serve as a source of understanding for people. When I was diagnosed in 2012, I knew no one with this disease. My mother's best friend's mother died from this disease. "It only affects older women," I told myself. "Surely this is just a misdiagnosis." But the more I learn about this disease and the more women I meet with ovarian cancer, the more I find a need to spread awareness—because 152,000 is too many. One is too many.

We live in a world where people glamorize being a cancer survivor, as they should! This is the toughest job, in my opinion. But what the world doesn't show you and the doctors don't tell you is that the hardest part of this job is navigating through life after the chemotherapy drip stops and the hospital visits come to a halt. You trade your patient wristband for your gold bangles. You're back at school or work and trying to carry on with everyday life. It'll never be the same. And I'm writing this for those of you facing a new diagnosis or trying to trek through life on the other side. It will get better. It won't be the same life you had before, but it'll be better. You will be stronger. And life does get sweeter.

My hope has always been to finish this damn book. *Ugh!* It's been so much harder than I ever thought. "Finish the book!" they said. "You must have so much to say!" I do have so much to say, but when you are finished with the treatment and finally have a glimpse at a "normal" life again, reliving it isn't always the first thing on the agenda. But, as anyone who has been through a cancer diagnosis and has lived to tell the tale will tell you, there's a reason we are still here today. I think my reason is to spread awareness and be the voice for those who are gone. Hopefully these stories can be a reminder for the next girl with cancer that she's not alone. Maybe the comments about being a teenager on a hall filled with people my grandparents' age will make her say, "I've been there!" Or maybe when she reads the part about not wanting to get up the next day and praying it was all a nightmare, she will now know that someone else has felt that similar pain in their heart. It's not the threat of suicide, but rather the everyday pain that you feel when you have cancer.

Tucked between the two covers of this book are the memories from my cancer journey. There is quite a bit of honesty, quite a bit of pain, and lots of love. I tried to gather my thoughts in a way that someone who has been through cancer or a difficult obstacle in life could relate to or appreciate. But I also wanted to share what it looked like from my point of view for those who were always curious: "What's it like to have cancer at nineteen?"

I used to struggle with the length of this book. I would measure my success with the number of pages I had written. It took me back to the days of high school, when we had page length requirements and I did the ol' "bait and switch" with the margins to stretch to one more page count. You can't forget to up the font size of the punctuation marks, too! Instead of trying to make this a lengthy book that compares to the others on the shelves next to it, I chose to just write, to write until I felt like the paragraph could make a difference. My favorite book I read during treatment was roughly seventy pages. Short and sweet. I learned more about the journey ahead and about myself than I did from any three-hundred-pager. After all, if there is one thing cancer survivors know to be precious, it's time.

These pages are chock-full of my story, my experience. I am so proud of the chance to share it with you.

# CHAPTER 3
# LIFE BEFORE

While I lay in my lofted bed in my freshman dorm room, my face just a few inches away from the foam ceiling tiles, I remember thinking about the week ahead, which was full of studying and preparation for exams. Anxiety regarding academics was always something I had kept at bay through high school. To be honest, it was always there, but I loved life too much to let those anxious feelings get in my way of having fun. Strong student? Sure! But more of a dreamer, really.

This was the first time I can recall ever feeling that I was experiencing a panic attack. As I lay there, I remember thinking of all of the plans my friends had drawn up for their future. Biology majors were heading to medical school, accounting majors were heading to graduate school, and so forth. Me? I was nowhere close to making a decision, and all I knew was business economics was my major. It sounded pretty good when I went home for Christmas break and told my family and friends what I was studying.

So I turned to my faith. I prayed that night to God that He would give me a sign: "Lord, please show me what I am supposed to do with my life. Please just give me a sign…positive or negative. I just need to know what I am to do with my life."

# CHAPTER 4
# SUMMER OF 2012

Fast-forward to midsummer. I was loving life as a nanny for two little girls, three and five years old, and our days were spent heading to "Easy Beach" and swimming at the pool. On my days off, I would rush down to the beach to get horizontal in the sand as quickly as I could. I loved the quiet time I had to myself, but my mind continued to race, even when there was no noise.

I attempted to push off any anxious feelings about returning to school and focusing on my future by working on my tan. I noticed that it became more and more difficult to lie in the sand on my stomach, so I resorted to looking like a flounder that summer. Tan on my front, pale on my back. I could tolerate only ten minutes in the sand on my stomach due to abdominal pain, which I passed off as gas pain. So I did what any normal nineteen-year-old would, and I popped a few Zantac and called it a day.

This went on for weeks without end. After a few more weeks of what I call "fart cramps," it was time to do some research. WebMD had never let me down before. So I saved myself the trouble of getting in the car and going to the doctor. I searched "gas cramps, bloating, and spotting" and received the following results: IBS, ovulation, appendicitis, ovarian cancer, and so forth. Well, it was obviously not ovarian cancer, since ovarian cancer is an older woman's disease. I quickly ruled that out. After missing a few days of my birth control pills and taking the forgotten ones all in one day, I attributed the spotting to my forgetfulness. Bloating was the result of good food and drinks and not having a set eating schedule, as I stayed busy with the girls running from one fun thing to the next and enjoying a meal when I could.

Who needs medical school? I had this thing all figured out. It was just a weird combination of several symptoms that could mean gloom and doom for someone else, but not me. How often do we do this in our own lives? We have clear signs from God that we need to address issues in front of us, but it's much easier to paint the picture we want rather than face reality.

Reality was the fourth result on WebMD—the result that I knew it just couldn't be.

*July 18, 2012*

I took a week off from nannying and joined Ragland, my boyfriend at the time, and his family at the beach for some rest and relaxation. On Monday of that week, my mother called with a reminder that I needed to head home Wednesday for my doctor's appointment that we scheduled earlier in the summer. I told her that I appreciated the reminder but would be rescheduling, as it did not fit in my schedule. My mother, who has always been a voice of reason, said it was best I get this appointment out of the way so I could enjoy the rest of the summer.

I headed home the following day to get back to town for my doctor's appointment on Wednesday.

This was to be a regular checkup with my new primary care physician. At nineteen, it was time to exit the pediatrician's office. I headed to my doctor's appointment the following morning with my bags in the car, ready to rejoin Ragland and his family at the beach after my well visit.

I was called back by the nurse, and, embarrassingly enough, my mother joined me for this visit. She stayed in the waiting room. Truth be told, I believe she joined me so that she knew I actually went to the doctor's appointment and didn't play hooky. As I made my way back to the exam room with the nurse, I remember thinking the last time I had a physical was during high school sports. As a rising sophomore in college, it seemed a little overkill. But hey, I aim to please, and what Mother says, I do.

The doctor came in and introduced herself. We chatted about all of the usual: school, career, exercise, eating habits, menstrual cycle. I told her that I had been taking birth control for a couple of years and had recently experienced spotting. When she asked just how long, I told her seventeen days. It wasn't until I said it aloud that I realized just how abnormal it was. She seemed a bit concerned, but I reassured her that I had missed a few birth control pills. The doctor then asked me to lie back on the exam table so that she could palpate my abdomen. As she worked her hands left and right, up and down, she began to look off into the distance, as if she were focusing. She continued to ask, "Any pain?"

As soon as the doctor touched one area in the lower left quadrant of my abdomen, I immediately flinched and told her that there was sensitivity there. Not wanting to show my full amount of discomfort, I told her it was painful, but not too bad. I watched her cup her hands as if she were scooping sand. She was cradling a lump in her hands.

Was I really seeing what I thought I was seeing? The doctor was cupping what looked to be a large bubble and seemed hard to the touch. She dug and dug until she was able to get a better grip on the "object." As I looked down to see what she was doing, the doctor asked me, "How long have you had this lump here?" Lump? Was she being serious? I began to nervously laugh and responded, "I didn't even know there was a lump."

I could tell in her expression that it was something concerning as she continued to poke and prod. She asked more questions about the bloating and spotting, and when I told her that both my mother and grandmother had ovarian cysts, I noticed her hardened face started to relax a bit. I have always prided myself on reading people, and I was relieved to see that she seemed comforted by that comment and that maybe this was simply an ovarian cyst.

The doctor requested a pregnancy test to rule out the obvious. As we waited for the test results, I remember sitting on the exam table thinking back on all of the times I had just turned over on the beach after experiencing some pain. The pressure I felt in my back when sunbathing on my stomach. The "fart cramps" that never went away with Zantac. The spotting that I attributed to missing birth control pills. Had I really neglected to address all of these issues after a few weeks of their presence?

The test was negative, and the doctor shared next steps would include an ultrasound the following day. When I asked her if we could reschedule, as I needed to get back to my week at the beach, she said to me, "Natalie, this is something that you shouldn't push off." She was right. I had done enough "pushing off," and it was time to face the inevitable.

I walked out to the waiting room where my mother was sitting, and she jumped up as she saw me walking toward her. She grabbed her purse and began walking out in front of me. I quickly started back in with the nervous laughter and told her that they had found a lump in my abdomen and that I needed to speak with the scheduler at the front desk to finalize my appointment the following day with radiology. My mother immediately began asking questions, and I could tell she was very concerned. Instead of speaking with the scheduler, my mother demanded a visit with the doctor herself. The scheduler was clear with my mother that since I was nineteen years old, my mother did not have access to my medical records. As my mother nearly pushed past the scheduler at the front desk, we made our way back to the same exam room I had been in moments before, and the doctor sat down with my mother and me to recap her findings.

The doctor shared that she was concerned and felt that we needed more information, which could be gathered from an ultrasound. She was vague and left us feeling hungry for more information. I look back now on those brief moments the three of us shared in that room together. I never realized just how precious those moments would be twenty-four hours later—some of the last moments I would have before my life would quickly change.

My ultrasound was scheduled for the following morning at 7:00 a.m. My father was in Florence for the workweek and drove in to town the night before. I remember calling him before he got in his car and saying that it was nothing to be concerned about. Dad told me on the phone that as Murphy's daughter, if he came to town, it would be nothing at all. Dad was always referred to as "Murphy," as in Murphy's Law, when we were younger. If something bad was going to happen, it was going to happen to Murphy. My first memory of this nickname sticking was when we were packing for a trip with my family, and my brother, Baxter, said to my dad, "Are you sure you don't need more bungee cords to hold the suitcases down on top of the car?" My dad reminded Baxter that he was a Boy Scout and had done this plenty of times before. Ten minutes down I-77, and my cousin Trent's Scooby-Doo underwear were being run over by an eighteen-wheeler.

*July 19, 2012*

My mom, dad, and I arrived at the hospital that morning for the ultrasound. I was called back just a few moments after sitting down in the waiting room. My mom came back with me, which I knew was her way of protecting me from possibly hearing any scary news alone. Only later did I realize why she needed to be there. As the ultrasound began, the tech moved the wand around the left side of my abdomen, where the tenderness and sensitivity was the day prior. I have no medical mind, but I knew when I saw a white bulb on the screen and the tech turn the computer away from my vision, she had spotted something concerning.

My mother began to ask the tech questions like, "Is that the right ovary? Where's the left ovary? Why can't you see the left ovary?" We would soon find out that what was hiding my left ovary was a tumor nearly the size of two grapefruits. The tumor had grown to encase the ovary, leaving little visibility for the tech to continue to perform the ultrasound. The tech would never share with us what her findings were but continued to deflect and share that "the doctor will call you with the results."

As the ultrasound tech handed me my cloth napkin to wipe the remaining ultrasound goo from my abdomen and thighs, she looked at both my mother and me with tear-filled eyes and said, "I will be praying for you."

Mom, Dad, and I got back in the car, and there was silence. As we drove back to the house, I knew in my heart that I needed to prepare for news that would change my life. This was not just an ovarian cyst. This was not spotting from taking too many birth control pills. This was not anything that I had planned for it to be.

After a roughly four-hour wait on a phone call from the doctor to share the results, my cell phone rang at 11:18 a.m. Cancer survivors will tell you that times and dates become very important in our lives. To most, the big and little hand on a clock can just mean the time of day. To survivors, those are defining points in our lives where our world is turned upside down.

I answered the phone, and my doctor from the day prior was on the phone. Her words were, "Natalie, this is Doctor X. I have the results from the ultrasound, and I would like you to please call your parents into the room. Put your phone on speaker, and sit down." Mom and Dad were already in the room when the phone rang, as we had been waiting with bated breath all morning long. Always priding myself on being a good reader of people, I could tell the calmness and intentionality in her voice was my sign, the sign that was to prepare me to hold on tight.

"What we believe Natalie to have is an ovarian tumor called dysgerminoma. The tumor is large. I am suggesting that we get you in with a gynecological oncologist who can specialize in the removal of this tumor and the treatment that may follow." Tumor? Large? Oncologist?

Everything around me went white. I had my dad on my right and my mom on my left at the kitchen table. My head just kept jerking back and forth between them. Their eyes were locked on each other and focusing on keeping their composure. I felt like I was in a foreign country and was trying to look at the locals for some help with translating what was being said to me. It was in this moment that the doctor shared comments that cemented the severity of this situation. "I am sorry to say that oftentimes, these tumors are malignant."

There it was. The comment that completely took my breath away. I couldn't catch it. I just sat there and began to take shallow breaths and rock back and forth. I immediately stood up and walked over to the couch to grasp what was being said over the phone. I was in need of space to feel like I could breathe. Isn't it strange that in moments where we receive difficult news that we run for air? When I think of receiving news like this, I think of clinging to those we love. But the reality was that I just needed to be alone. I needed to digest the phone call and process it on my own. The call continued for several minutes, with my parents rattling off questions as quickly as they could think of them all while keeping their cool.

"Where do we go from here? Is this the best gynecological oncologist in Charleston? Can we go in for lab work this afternoon? How big was the tumor exactly?"

While my parents continued their questions, I sat on our green couch in the den and stared into the doorway of my bedroom that connected to the rest of the house. The sun was shining in through the windows in my room. Just the day before, I went for a run on the beach. Just the day before, I was swimming in the ocean. Just the day before, I felt that sun on my face. In this moment, all I could focus on was the whiteness of my room from the light. I was stuck in a gaze, like one of those times when you can't break your stare, no matter how hard you try. I heard the conversations around me but could not contribute to any of it. I was losing control. All I could say was, "Lord, please."

When the phone call ended, my parents came over to the couch and embraced me in a hug. The three of us sat there and held each other. No words were spoken, as I now realize the fear that I had must have paled in comparison to the fear that they were facing, knowing that their child was in danger and they were witnesses with no way to help. I cried for a few minutes and gasped for air. I had moments where I would make no noise but would feel my body convulsing from the terror of what was to come. The next moment, I was staring at the light in my room. Calm, quiet, focused.

I began to gather myself and stepped out on to our front porch. I reached for my phone to call Ragland and share the news with him. Before I dialed, I struggled with what to say. Do I own what the doctor had just shared? Do I jump to the other side and choose denial? It was my first introduction to the identity crisis that I believe many cancer patients face at some point in their journey. I chose to reveal as little information as possible so that I did not alarm him over the phone. I wanted him with me, in front of me, so that he could see I was okay and that I was choosing to be strong.

How do you tell someone you love information that you know will upset them? Hell if I knew.


*July 23, 2012*
The night before the scheduled surgery can only be described as the adrenaline rush that a football

player must feel before playing in the Super Bowl. I felt a sense of calmness and peace over me as it became later and later in the evening. I grabbed my orange soap and lathered up as they instruct you before any surgery. No lotion, no products. Just suds up with this orange product until you look jaundiced. The shower was the last time I could have my thoughts to myself. I stood in the shower and ran through my thoughts in my head. What would tomorrow be like? Should I cry now? Will I cry tomorrow? Do I need to tell people goodbye? Should I have written a will?

I prepared for the surgery in about the same manner as my shoulder surgery in high school: this sucks, and I am going to be down and out for a few days. Now, on the other side, what an underestimated view of an ovarian tumor removal surgery! I'll get to that later. Before the sun went down, we went on a family golf cart ride around the island. There was an odd peace to this ride that I cannot quite explain. I recall holding my stomach as if I were pregnant. It was as if I was afraid that I might deliver the tumor with each pothole that we hit. We returned home to a quiet house that would soon grow even quieter as the clock moved closer to bedtime. As I took my last few sips of water before the midnight cutoff, I kissed my parents goodnight. Mom and Dad allowed Ragland to sleep on the daybed in my room that night. I'm not sure why, as that was never allowed in the Hahn house. Maybe it was because they knew I needed the comfort of just having someone in arms' distance.

We all said prayers in my room that night and prayed for peace, for steady hands, and for our family to choose faith, not fear. After Mom, Dad, Bax, and the dogs all left the room, Ragland lay on the edge of the bed until I fell asleep. Before I drifted off, Ragland and I had an honest conversation that I wished our nineteen-year-old selves didn't have to have. I told Ragland that just because this was something I was facing in my life, it did not mean he had to face it. When you love someone, you love them enough to set them free from something that may cause them pain. The worst thing I could do was make Ragland be a witness to the pain and possibly loss.

There are moments in people's relationships where they say, "I knew the exact moment I wanted to marry him." This was my moment. Ragland did not hesitate for a second. He responded by telling me he was with me for the long haul. No matter what we faced, he would be there. I mean, swoon! Love is a beautiful thing. I drifted off to sleep and slept like a baby. I had an army of people behind me, beside me, and in front of me. And God was over me.

*July 24, 2012*

One of the benefits of having a tumor the size of two grapefruits growing out of your left ovary that grows 40 percent over the weekend is you get pushed to the first surgery spot of the day. We were all up before the sun began to rise as we arrived to check in at the hospital. After check-in, we sat in the waiting room until I was called back to change into my hospital gown and cap. Mom went back with me to get me situated before they began the premeds. She hung a sign around my neck that read, "I get very, very sick with anesthesia (projectile vomiting)"—a preventative measure so that everyone who I came in contact with knew how much care and attention I would need. After a shoulder surgery in high school that sent me puking for days, we were not taking any chances. Little did we know this would be the least of our concerns. Once I was settled, they allowed family to come back so that we could all be together one last time before surgery. The doctors came in and each did their introduction. They gave us the rundown of what to expect, how long I would be in surgery, and what our plan of action was in the final moments before I was rolled back. The nurse anesthetist was very friendly, and it was as if I was her new puppy. She patted my head and rubbed my arm while saying such kind and comforting words. This was something my parents needed to see. They needed to witness that, although they were having to let go, someone else was there to grab hold.

The time came when it was my turn to be pushed back. The nurse anesthetist told me she would be pushing some medicine that would help me relax. I wouldn't remember much after we would go through the double doors. We took this as our cue to say goodbye. Before I lost consciousness, we all shared "I love yous" and "See you soons." Not one tear was shed until the good stuff was pushed as my bed became unlocked and we started rolling. I looked up to the ceiling as we rolled and passed several nurses. The solemn look on their faces made me sad. I knew where I was going, and they did too.

When a surgery that is to last roughly three hours runs into six hours, it's concerning. Mom and Dad received an update halfway through by my doctor, who shared that the cancer had spread further than we thought. Left ovary, right ovary, a few lymph nodes, washings, and pelvic wall. The decision was made by Mom and Dad to leave my right ovary in the hopes that the chemotherapy would do the job and rid my body of any remaining cancer. I was moved to an area for patients coming off anesthesia, where my family was brought in. As I started to wake up, I heard Dad, Ragland, and Bax standing over my bed. Dad said, "Hey, Nattie Girl, all done! You did it!"

I've always been a no-bullshit kind of gal. I needed to cut to the chase. I asked Dad, with eyes closed, "Was it malignant?" There was a pause, and he said, "Yes, ma'am, it was." No pause on my part. "F—— cancer!" I yelled in the recovery room. (I stop at *F*, as I hope to sell this in bookstores one day, but the full word was proclaimed.) Just as I shared my thoughts on this disease, a doctor walked to the foot of my bed and told me he agreed with my thoughts exactly. And really, what else is there to say? You're a nineteen-year-old with stage 3C ovarian cancer. *F—— cancer* is right.

# CHAPTER 5
# CANCER DIAGNOSIS FOR A YOUNG WOMAN

I think back to some of my obstacles before cancer, and I wonder how in the world I ever lost sleep over some things. It's comical to me that I allowed myself to stress over such small things in life, but I realize that's how the rest of the world sees life too. If you are privileged enough to see life in the most beautiful way (through the eyes of a cancer patient), you'll understand what I mean by that. This can be true for anyone who has experienced a major health scare in their lifetime. People who walk away scot-free from terrible car accidents say the same thing. "I see life differently now. I've been given a second chance." Try that approach, and put it on steroids. There's something really beautiful about a cancer diagnosis and the way it changes your life. But, damn, it is hard to see that in the middle of the storm!

When I was first diagnosed, I searched high and low for books about young women battling cancer. I was in need of some kind of guidebook to help me manage my new membership in a club I wanted nothing to do with. I couldn't find a thing. So I explored other books about younger women battling breast cancer and parents of pediatric cancer patients and their memoirs. Nothing seemed to really relate to my situation, so the idea to write my own book was born.

Facing cancer as a young woman is a sick reality that you are quickly losing control of your own life. At a time when we strive for control and success, cancer just sweeps right in and steals what independence you have. I often found myself in a power struggle between wanting to do things myself and begging someone to help me. I was scared, and honestly, I just wanted other people to tell me what to do. I was afraid to navigate this world alone because when you receive a cancer diagnosis at nineteen, that's exactly how you feel: alone.

*How to Share the News*

Out of all of the shelves in Barnes & Noble, you would think there would be at least one book, maybe even a pamphlet, on how to tell people in your life the news that you might have cancer. Not one. Zilch. None.

So I blindly entered this next chapter of the journey with probably a similar approach to how I entered my exams freshman year of college…hoping for the best. The conversation with Ragland went about as well as you can imagine. It led to lots of questions and some silences, which I knew was just him trying to find the right words to say. This is the guy that always filled the awkward silences. He always had something funny to say that made me laugh or made me remember what was important. In this moment, we changed roles, and I recall telling him that I would be okay and that it was not the freshman fifteen or a "food baby" that I had really been banking on, but rather a tumor. There were times where I could tell that

Ragland was trying his best to phrase his words in the kindest way possible, but even he had a suspicion that there was something going on causing my weight gain. "At least all of that exercise was probably working! This tumor was just making me look bad!"

When people know you well, they can quickly determine when you are overcompensating. It didn't take long for Ragland to jump in the car and make it to Charleston within the hour. While we waited for him to arrive, my parents and I all took turns returning phone calls to family who had been praying for clear results from the ultrasound after being alerted the night before of the situation at hand. I called friends who were praying and sent text messages.

Let's get one thing straight. Text messages are not the appropriate delivery mode for borderline cancer diagnoses, okay? Take it from me, who sent her college girls' group chat a paragraph about the tumor that they found. Pick up the damn phone and talk to people. One by one. "I don't have much information, but what I do know is _____." It's your story. Own it. Do not let your friends' minds wander as they try and decipher words like "dys-germinoma" and "germ cell." My girls are some of the most intelligent women I know, but even those words are scary to them. Even the biology majors. Let them hear your voice because they are also experiencing a life-altering diagnosis.

Really, it's all about timing. You have to take the proper amount of time to process the news. My family and I created lists of people that needed to be contacted, and that seemed to be a good approach for us. The burden was never on me to share the news with people. It was only if I wanted to make those calls. As the day went on, I found myself having calmer conversations with family and friends. The later in the day, the more rehearsed I became on the phone, and I realized that my confidence was growing. I was taking control of the situation and owning my story.

*Owning Your Story*

Before you make the call to others about what your doctor has shared with you, think about how you feel. It is perfectly normal to ask the question, "Why me?" In fact, let it simmer for a bit. You may have heard about the five stages of grief. I think this applies to a cancer diagnosis. Maybe not all five, but I can pinpoint moments in my journey where these hit home. Denial, anger, bargaining, depression, and acceptance. I hit all five of these within the first ten minutes of hearing the news that the doctors had found a tumor that was possibly malignant. I found that the sooner that I accepted my diagnosis, the faster I would see the light at the end of the tunnel.

This is *your* story. No cancer diagnosis is the same, and do not ever let someone belittle your pain and struggle with the comment "I know how you feel." (This will be addressed later, as this one line could use its own chapter.) This is your moment to feel how you want to feel and what is natural. Assess your reaction to the news, and own it.

Process your life, and realize where you stand in this moment. You have been given a diagnosis, and you will not have definitive information until surgery. But what you do know is that the doctors are concerned. This is the prequel to your cancer journey. From the moment I answered the phone at 11:18 a.m., I was a cancer survivor. I was beginning to write the story of my journey with cancer, and like all good actors and actresses, they prepare a short speech before accepting an award on stage. So I grabbed my pen and paper and jotted down all that I knew to be true before talking to anyone so that I felt composed and in control. Being in control during this phase is key.

*Sharing and Preparing*

I do not think I was prepared for the number of concerned responses we would receive as the news was shared. In fact, I think I was probably so caught off guard that I did not get to fully share what I wanted with each person I contacted. I was so taken aback by the offers to help that I forgot some of my talking points. When you share your news with others, be prepared to have responses to questions like "What can I do? When is surgery? Who is the doctor? Do you want me to call so-and-so?"

My suggestion: Always have a response for when people ask what they can do. "Thank you! Continued prayers for comfort and healing." "I could use some fresh air. Would you come and walk with me?" "I read somewhere that soft clothes are nice to wear after surgery. Would you please go to Target and pick up a few things?"

Responses to the questions regarding treatment can come later. In the meantime, my go-to response is "I've shared with you all that I know, but we should know more when we meet with the doctor."

### Understanding Others' Reactions

Being completely candid here. I would get hot and bothered by people who would cry when I shared the news. I did not understand how people could be selfish enough to sulk in their own sadness when they were not the ones preparing for battle. How wrong was I? What I did not see through my cancer blinders was that every person you share your story with is entitled to their own individual reaction to the news. I used to think, "If I'm not crying, they shouldn't be crying!" or "Why do I have to comfort them? They should be comforting me! This is exhausting!" I believe God places emotional people in our lives for several reasons. For instance:

**For strength.** By comforting others during a difficult time you are experiencing yourself, it exposes your own strength that you may not have realized you had all along.

**For purpose.** It reminds us of the purpose that we cancer warriors play in their lives. This is a wonderful reminder that we have a purpose and that we can be in control, even when we may feel we are spiraling right out of it.

**For love.** When you love someone, you care so deeply about them, and you hurt when they hurt. The tears that are shed for you are all from a strong foundation of love.

Strength, purpose, and love were three traits that I strived to find in myself during my journey. Having these three marked off in my mind allowed me to really understand and digest my diagnosis, and therefore, I could share in the emotions that my family and friends were experiencing.

*Choosing Your Path*

When I share my diagnosis story with people, I often find myself emphasizing those "few minutes" that I cried right after hearing the news. I try to highlight that it was truly just for a few minutes. It was in those first moments of hearing the news that I may have cancer that I had control. Not many people feel that they have control during the hours that follow a grave diagnosis, but I grabbed on to whatever I could to feel strong.

There are two paths to take with a cancer diagnosis. You can either choose to be strong or choose to let the disease overtake you. Cancer is just as much of an emotional disease as it is physical. There is no right or perfect way to handle cancer being woven into your life because cancer is the most imperfect thing. It just is. Cancer doesn't play by the rules. It does not care what age you are, what color you are, or how rich or poor you are. In fact, it seems to come at the most inopportune times. At least, that's how it feels, at first.

All of the self-help books cannot help you choose what path you are going to take, but I hope and encourage you to take the high road: facing cancer head-on. I often pictured cancer as a person because I felt like I had strength to take on a body, something tangible. Telling myself to take on something that had no real form seemed like

I wasn't giving myself a fair description of what cancer really is. So I chose to visualize the disease in human form. One nurse offered to cover my IV pole that held my chemotherapy with a blanket so that I might forget that it was there and hopefully "get some rest." I told her it was fine to remain in sight and, in fact, she should probably push it closer to me so that I could really stare at it.

Once you choose your path and decide which route you will take, it's therapeutic to share with those that you love just which approach will be yours. This allows our friends and family to properly arm themselves with the right ammunition to help us fight the disease.

# CHAPTER 6
# CANCER POSSE

When you receive a cancer diagnosis, it's inevitable that many people you know, or maybe do not know, will come forward to share their personal experience with the disease. It took me some time, but I realized just how therapeutic this was for friends and family to relive some of their diagnosis journey. In fact, I find myself doing that today. There is not a person I meet who has been diagnosed with whom I don't feel inclined to share some insight or a helpful tip.

These amazing individuals who surrounded me with such knowledge and strength are the group I called my cancer posse. These were women who had known the fear that came with hearing the words "You have cancer." They, too, had been given a hospital gown to change into and asked to lie on a cold exam table while they ponder their lives in the silence. They knew the "puking after chemo" stomach pains that one feels after bile passes through your body when there is nothing left. Neuropathy was their new normal, just like mine. If anyone was allowed to say, "I know how you feel," it was these women.

Having a strong cancer posse allowed me to get the real answers I looked for during my treatment. A dear friend and fellow member of the cancer posse, Flora Anne, once told me, "They are pumpin' actual poison into ya body, so if ya in pain, honey, it's workin'." Honesty is always the best policy with cancer patients as we strive to gain control of what we can and to never be surprised by any symptom or scare.

Building your cancer posse is important because it allows you to have a separate support group, which is different than family and friends. As wonderful as your family is, sometimes not understanding the severity of the pain or sickness you are feeling can drive a wedge between you and those you love. I recall trying to explain to my parents one day that I just couldn't eat even one bite of food. After nearly everyone was in tears, it was time for a cancer posse member to speak up and tell everyone to back off. "She'll eat when she wants to eat!" they would say. "Give her ice cream! Go get her Arby's." Bless these amazing women who choose to go back to the lions' den and be reminded of their own battles. These women are survivors for a reason.

# CHAPTER 7

# UNDERSTANDING YOUR FAMILY

I stand by my remarks made early in my cancer journey. It is always easier to go through it than to watch someone you love go through it. I hope to have the joy one day of becoming a parent and knowing the love for someone you helped create. Now, imagine that person you helped create is being attacked, and there is nothing that you can do to help. Enter Mom and Dad, stage right.

Priding yourself on having the ability to read people and understand their body language without saying a word comes with a price. That price was pain for me. It hurt to watch my parents process the news, just as much as it hurt me to know I would be going through it. Seeing Baxter's and Ragland's faces for the first time postsurgery after the anesthesia had worn off and knowing that their lives would drastically change pained me. Just as we have to deal with understanding friends' reactions, we have to process our family's response to it all.

My brother and I were always homebodies growing up. When my mother would drop us off at Mother's Morning Out, we were always uneasy at first. Who are these strange people she has left us with? Where is she going? Why can't we just go with her? I was my most comfortable on my parents' hips as a little girl.

When I think of those early moments in my cancer diagnosis, I picture myself at Mother's Morning Out, except the roles are reversed. I picture my parents in my place and me in theirs. I am walking out the door, not able to explain to them that I will be fine and that I will return. But they are so upset to even hear or process the news. Imagine feeling the pain that we homebodies felt as children—except you feel it as an adult, and you are aware of what is happening. Time is real, and it seems to be slipping away every second.

I had honest and real conversations with my family during my cancer journey. We talked about life and about death. We talked about what we thought heaven is like and what music we would want played at our funerals. Strictly Motown jams was my request. "Happy music only!" I told them. I love to think about what heaven must be like, and I enjoy hearing from others how they picture the next life. I picture heaven to be a huge party. When you arrive, you have a moment of solace. There, you are met by Jesus. You are welcomed. He tells you about your life and ties up loose ends for you. "Remember when you didn't get that job you so desperately wanted and could never figure out why? That had to happen so that you could meet so-and-so, who would hire you for your dream job." Things like that. Little things that make you realize how important prayer is in your life. Then, he takes you to this banquet hall, where you are greeted by a long table that is filled with every food you can imagine. Around the table is every person you've ever loved in your life. Pets too! I've never thought past this moment. And honestly, I don't think I can imagine anything greater than this. But I know there is so much more beyond that banquet hall.

Talking about where we go after we die was an integral part of my healing. We never let those conversations fizzle out, as they were often the root of my anxiety and pain. It was important to feel like I had an outlet, and being as candid with them as I could be was healthy. The same goes for providing my loved ones with an outlet. When my parents would show their emotions, I would have the opportunity to be strong. I enjoyed having just Baxter and Ragland in the room because this always guaranteed comic relief. These are two of the funniest people I know. The boys always chose humor to cope, and I find that my choice of a coping mechanism is laughing too.

The doctors encouraged my parents to allow family to suggest questions we might ask the care team. This allowed open lines of communication and would cut down on the telephone game that almost always occurs when you have a sudden health concern in the family. When Baxter learned that my left ovary would be removed, he asked if I would PMS every other month now. Honest questions from the mouth of a man. Granting family the chance to inquire allows a sense of control, which is such a gift during a cancer journey.

I realized that a major part of this book reaching those affected by cancer and their loved ones was for all angles of the story to be told. Over the next few pages, you'll hear from my parents, Baxter, and Ragland on a few of their takeaways. I asked them to document their initial emotions as best as they could recall. There is a story to be told from the parents, brother, and boyfriend of the girl with cancer. They deserve to be heard and understood. After all, it's much easier to be the one fighting than the one watching the fight.

*My Mom, Tracy:*

When told in recovery that the mass was malignant, Natalie said, "F—— cancer." That was that. Cancer had picked on the wrong girl! I no longer saw a groggy and weak child lying in a hospital bed; I saw a three-year-old fiercely independent and willful child. My mind flashed back to a conversation I had with my dad some sixteen years earlier. He said, "Don't break her spirit. It will serve her well." Daddy, she's gonna need that *now*!

The doctor wanted to talk with Big Baxter and me outside of the operating room, about three hours into the surgery. She confirmed that the cancer had not only enveloped the right ovary, but cancer was on the left ovary as well. The doctor wanted to know if we wanted to remove the unexpected cancerous ovary as well. The room was getting hot. My shirt was getting tighter. I found it hard to breathe. We discussed the two options: take it or leave it. She was only nineteen! Barren at nineteen? Make that decision for her? After consulting with another gyn-onc in that small corridor, we made the decision for our daughter. The other ovary was left with the hopes that chemotherapy would do its job. If not, the cancerous ovary could be removed arthroscopically at a later date. It was getting hotter. Pray. Sounds were really loud. I could feel the sounds in my head. Baxter was ushering me through the double doors when he pointed to a woman carrying a tray of sandwiches, a basket of food, and a cooler. Gosh, it was hot! Baxter said to her, "You. Here." He grabbed a chair. It was my dear friend Marion into whose arms I collapsed. Cancer was discovered in the washings and lymph nodes. A spot on her pelvic wall had been discovered, biopsied, and confirmed malignant upon closing.

After surgery, Baxter and I met with the doctor in a conference room. Natalie would begin chemotherapy in three weeks. The doctor looked tired. The surgery lasted longer than anticipated. The doctor was a new mother. She understood! Baxter and I prayed together for our daughter's healing. We prayed alone. We prayed with friends. We prayed in Stella Maris Church as Father McInerney administered the sacrament, Anointing of the Sick, to our Natalie. We prayed while walking the beach.

CaringBridge gave us the opportunity to keep our loving family and friends informed. This was a tremendous vehicle to share updates and even feelings. Each family member and Ragland took turns writing these updates. Even Natalie wrote some! That Ragland...we nicknamed him "Elmer" (like the glue). He was our glue at times. He surfed, talked, and biked with Bax IV, entertained Natalie, carried coolers and groceries, sat with Natalie, played with the dogs, and cheered on Natalie!

Natalie's chemo regimen was arduous. She was to be in the hospital for five to six days receiving three different chemo drugs intravenously. Imagine a nineteen-year-old in a hospital room for that length of time every three weeks for four sessions. She would have lab work done upon checking into the hospital. Her chemo drugs would be prepared and then administered. This took hours! She wouldn't even begin the first treatment until suppertime. That of course, pushed back the discharge until late the sixth day or early morning hours of the seventh day. This was going to be burdensome to all involved. We managed to make changes for subsequent treatments by checking into the hospital late in the day for the necessary lab work. Once completed, Natalie and I would sneak out of the hospital on the pretense of getting some fresh air before the port was accessed. "Welcome to Moe's!" is what we heard after we hightailed it over to have supper on King Street.

Another formidable problem with the extended chemo treatments was the depressing atmosphere of the hospital room. Because one of the chemo drugs kept her confined to the tiled floor of the hospital room, visits to the family dayroom were forbidden. That was not acceptable. We decided to decorate the hospital room with different themes for each stay. I first thought of this as a way to help Natalie get through a tough week. I was surprised at the positive effect it had on me, the staff, and visitors.

During the first week of treatment, sleeping in the chair beside her bed in that dreadful hospital room, so many dark thoughts haunted me. One desperate night, I wrote in my spiral notebook that I kept to document drugs and times, "*We have all made requests to You that are going unanswered. Did You hear? Do You listen?*"

The next day, I stopped at the grocery store to pick up a few things on the way home from the hospital. It was Baxter's night to stay. That's how we did it. We took turns. The grocery store might make me feel "normal," like I'm not in the middle of this horrible nightmare, watching my daughter fight for her life. I dreaded the thought of running into someone who knew of Natalie's illness. Well, I ran into some unfortunate soul who asked about Natalie and said she was praying for her. My heart was raw with pain. I snapped back at her saying, "I'm glad you are praying for Natalie because God isn't listening to me!" There! I'd said out loud what was gnawing at my heart! I couldn't believe I'd said that and just kept pushing that buggy. That night, while in the shower, I cried. I cried a lot in the shower. I was alone. Baxter was at the hospital with Natalie. Young Baxter was back at college. The dogs didn't know what was going on. I loved taking those hot showers! The next day, I was walking on the beach with the dogs. Normal. I talked with God on my walks. He didn't talk back. That next night at the hospital, with only the light from the IV stand, I wrote the following:

*"I am feeling so much hurt and anger. I am tired of living like this. I give up. I am giving it ALL to You! Please heal my hurting heart. I don't understand! It takes me a while, but I can see that You are using THIS for Your glory and my good! I'm glad I was honest with You, myself, and my friend in the grocery store."*

I had laid my heart open to God for Him to enter. It was at that time that I also allowed friends to help. I had mistakenly pushed friends and family away, thinking, *I've got this. I'm the mother. I'm in control.* They brought food, visited, and showered us with love and prayers.

I began to see the results of letting go, letting God, and letting in. The bonds with my friends and family became stronger, and my faith became deeper. I remember sitting on the beach with Melita, something I wouldn't have done a week before, when I realized my bathing suit bottom was inside out. Yes, the white liner was just out there, for all to see. We laughed and laughed. God, I needed that! I was thanking God for that brief moment of fun. Other moments of fun and faith began to fill and heal my raw heart.

If God had this, then I was all in! I was OK with being in control of being positive! He had a lot of work to do! There! I was in control…of something!

*My Dad, Baxter:*
Dealing with a child who has been diagnosed with cancer and how that impacts a father is something

that could be described as entering a different realm. I wondered if, after hearing the news and full diagnosis, this was perhaps how a soldier feels when an explosion goes off near them. I remember looking around with my ears ringing, wondering if, in fact, something had happened to me. Strange as that sounds, it was like being shell-shocked, where your body moves but you don't know where to go or what to do. I recall trying to gather myself because, as a father, you hope that the rest of the family gauges you and looks for your stability. It took a while for me to find that...a long time.

I do remember spiraling into a hopeless period where I felt no control and that life had decided that I was going to be one of those people who would lose their father at a young age, only to possibly lose my daughter and how terrible this was going to be. Would I make it through this? How would the rest of the family react to all of this? The low was one morning when Tracy and I lay in bed crying off and on through the night in the Coxes' house at Litchfield Beach. This was shortly after Natalie's surgery to remove the tumor and before we knew how bad it really was. Well, Litchfield is a special place for me, and I know that I was there for a reason. You see, this is the place I hold wonderful memories. As a child we always vacationed at Pawley's, Litchfield, and Garden City.

I was standing that morning, having slept very little, looking out over the ocean and recalling how my dad would put me on his shoulders and walk through the waves. He was bald, and it was always hard for me to hold on to his head while on his shoulders! Those were special times. I think that when you find yourself in a difficult spot, people often reflect back to those times where life was innocent and problems were nonexistent. I pleaded deeply to my father, who had passed away thirty-three years earlier, to please help. I felt in some ways that if I prayed hard enough, he would do something. I remember getting mad, stomping the sand, demanding that he step up and help for once! I was a desperate person who was completely void of ideas of how I was going to get Natalie out of this situation.

Then I started walking…and I said I would walk for thirty minutes up the beach and thirty minutes back. The only difference was I would pray the entire way, up and down the beach. This was harder than I thought, as my mind was racing, trying to find a way out of this situation for Natalie. Upon returning back at the beach house, I had a strange, very strange, feeling that came over me. I was crying really hard, and I was the most open and vulnerable I had ever been, and this feeling just swept over me. I felt the Lord get angry with me. Not as if I had never really asked for His help, but more like I had never really listened to Him. He said that He had this situation and that He owned it and would take care of things, but I had to "get on board"—I remember that term distinctly. It was like, "I've got this, but you better get on board and believe." At that moment I turned around and walked up the walkway, and the term "Faith, Not Fear" came to me. I walked inside the house with most everyone up for the day and said, "We are going to embrace 'Faith, Not Fear.'" And it was as if everyone thought, "Well, where the heck has that been the whole time?"

Some of the things that come from a crisis such as this is the discovery of how your friends and family genuinely feel about you. To see the outpouring of love and support is one thing from those closest to you, but to witness what we saw through Natalie's illness was truly amazing. Natalie started traveling the state and sharing her story with others shortly after her treatment stopped. She speaks about the power of a strong community in one of her speeches that says something like, "If you were one of those people that greeted my Mom or Dad in the third aisle of the Harris Teeter with nothing more than a full-arms hug, I say thank you. You were the energy that got us through this." These people are never quite the same to you again. They are family. I'm sure it's what soldiers feel after going through battle together or how neighbors comfort others after hurricanes and storms. There is no black, no white, no rich or poor. You totally drop your guard and come to assist, and that is what we felt dealing with Natalie's crisis. Our family grew exponentially. What a gift to all of us.

Lastly, with all the benefits listed and discussed in these sentences, it's important to know that there is a flip side to this and that is one thrust upon all of us, but most especially Natalie. That is the inability to ever fully rest. What I mean is that you are now always on watch. No matter what the doctors say or medical evidence proves, you always remain on careful watch. Knowing full well the evidence proves that she has advanced out of that crisis zone, we all still remain on respectful watch. Like a night watchman trained to "stay alert," our family will never really rest. But for that small amount of discomfort, we celebrate her beating this potentially fatal illness with her complete, unending *Nattitude.*

*My Husband, Ragland:*

When Natalie called me…I basically got to tell my mom that there was a "mass" found in my girlfriend's abdomen. When my mom asked me if we thought she may be pregnant, I said, "I don't think so." I, on the other hand, had a churning in my stomach that Natalie may be sick. I knew she wasn't pregnant, but it certainly was my first thought.

The next morning, Natalie called me and told me it was a tumor, and I learned what *benign* and *malignant* meant. I was at the beach about an hour north from Natalie at the time. After putting on a good face for my parents as I shared the news with them, I got into bed and cried like a baby. There were lots of little teary episodes, but I had to have a strong face in front of Natalie. There were two events that stand out that were not "a little teary."

In bed that night, I'll never forget the prayers I said. I prayed that God would take my life instead of hers. And I said that over and over. I noticed that my tears were honestly not for pity on myself asking such a thing, but more of passion, of how badly I wanted my life taken instead of hers. I've still never told her I prayed this, as it could seem aggressive. However, ever since, I've always wondered if that prayer could still be answered by God down the road...like I picture myself doing something really fun (like rollerblading or something) and God just pops in and is like, "Oh yeah, remember that time I didn't take Natalie's life? Here's a stick for you to blade over." Although I'm being funny with this example, I always use this as a reminder of how precious life is.

The following morning was Sunday, and I attended the church where my dad was working as an assistant rector. He was in seminary at the time and got a summer job at a church near our beach house. The news had spread that it was a tumor, and on my way out of the church, the pastor held both of my shoulders and looked me in the eye and very causally told me, "She's going to be OK." In my mind I replied, "OK, dude, you better be right..." His words made me feel better.

I cranked my car in the parking lot to head down, and the battery was clearly not cooperating. Not liking to be the center of attention and certainly not wanting the soothsaying pastor to help me, I didn't ask anyone for help and rather just said a prayer. It somehow cranked. I turned off the AC and the stereo to preserve battery and luckily made it to Advance Auto Parts. The manager helped me install the battery since I'm a super handyman myself...I had to tell someone that something was churning in my stomach. I sarcastically told him about how great the timing of the dead battery was as I was heading down to see my girlfriend after they found a tumor in her abdomen. He told me he would pray for me, as he had been through a similar situation. I cranked the car to head down to see Natalie, and Josh Turner's song came on the radio, and as I turned up the volume, I heard the lyrics "Right now she's where I need to be."

As for the second time I cried really hard: After Natalie's surgery, I watched the doctor tell Natalie's parents the tumor was malignant. I was out of ear-shot to hear the news, but their reaction made it clear. I then began my nickname of Natalie's cancer story, "Elmer." The glue that held her family together. I had to be positive and keep the family calm. I put on a really good face and tried to keep everyone positive in the waiting room after the surgery. However, deep down, I was dying.

On my way to their beach house when I was in my car alone, I got a call from our friend, Cleburne Fant. I remember right where I was. I was exiting off the Ravenel Bridge toward Sullivan's Island. I didn't want to pick up because I was emotional, and I thought he was, like many people, wanting to be the first to know if it was benign or malignant. For some reason, I picked up. "Hey, Rags, I know it's been a rough day. Is it OK if I say a prayer for you?" I'm tearing up writing this because I remember how tough it was to hold back tears…so I didn't. I sprayed my speedometer with tears right away and muttered a "yes." He prayed for a little longer than was comfortable, given the fact that I was driving and was unable to see straight due to the tears. He prayed for Natalie, her family, the doctors, and care techs, and then me. When he got to me, I realized how difficult all of the treatment plan was actually going to be for me. When he said "Amen," I tried to say thank you, but I don't even know if I got it out audibly before hanging up. I still to this day haven't confirmed with him if he knew how much I appreciated that or if he thought I was being rude just hanging up on him. I think he knew. I cried so hard during that phone call, but realized some of it was pity on myself. I stopped and pulled myself together and told myself, "That's the end of that." Imagine what Natalie was feeling…

During Natalie's treatment, I didn't know if I was doing well as "the boyfriend." One night, I embarrassingly researched "how to help my girlfriend just diagnosed with cancer." The first thing that popped up was a forum where someone asked about the same question I typed. Except he finished it with "I think I should just break up with her." That's when I realized Natalie and I were on a different wavelength than others. We were much closer and much more in love than this loser. That was so far from how I felt...to the extent that I knew I would marry her one day.

Trust me, after watching her hair come out and grow back, I'll never resent my wife's hair getting in my mouth during a kiss, or when it takes way too long to get it looking pretty before we go out for dinner.

*My Brother, Baxter:*

My sister and I are Irish twins (sixteen months apart, to be exact). I'm not sure if it's because of our closeness in age, but I have always felt like my sister and I were in each other's brain. I had a silly worry when I was younger that she somehow had a back door to my thoughts. I did not want to keep a secret from her for fear she could somehow find it. One day, we were so convinced that we had some version of sibling ESP, we agreed to count down from three and shout the first animal that came to mind. We did not match up on the first or eighth try, but we were not any less confident.

So, when Natalie was diagnosed and had to spend a week at a time in the hospital, I knew we (I) needed to be strong because I knew Natalie would be coming in the back door to see what was actually going on! So I needed to be positive and only have good thoughts. Natalie would find that bad thought if there was one.

I found that staying busy was the key to helping Natalie fight and heal. I remember visiting the registrar's office multiple times to print an official transcript to prepare for my transfer to the Darla Moore School of Business to be closer to home. I called my parents numerous times saying, "I'm doing it! Can't stand being five hours away. Y'all need help." But they insisted I stay at Wake Forest and that everything was under control. It was, but I felt like I needed to be around. On one particular visit home, Natalie asked an exhausting number of questions about school. She was totally dissecting my junior year, and I realized that she was, for a short time, living vicariously through me. She asked colorful questions that would really give her the sense of being there. I realized that keeping things as normal as possible was the key. Had I transferred home, she would have sensed something very wrong. I had to keep those positive thoughts coming!

Sometimes, it was hard to stay positive. I remember my parents and I would often snap at each other when staying alone at Believe Inn. We certainly could not snap or break down in front of Natalie, so this is where we did it. I remember a summer thunderstorm that sent both dogs scrambling into the other room, spilling my drink. I yelled at them to calm down. I do not know why this incident stuck with me, but it has. I was yelling at the dogs because they did not understand the storm. They did not understand that it would pass, that it would not eat us alive, that it was a natural happening. When I was scared during Natalie's sickness, I was my dogs. I was cowering in fear because of something I did not understand. Once I left the battle in God's hands, those thunderstorms were not as scary. I did not need to run into another room and cower under the bed. He had it under control. It was His will, anyway!

We have come a long way from printing out transcripts to transfer colleges. Last year, I printed out an official transcript from Wake Forest to apply for my International Masters of Business Administration at the Darla Moore School of Business. After being deemed cancer-free, Natalie would come to visit me while I was living and working in Paris! We had a blast! I was able to show her all my favorite gardens, see the magnificent works of art in la Louvre and le Musée d'Orsay, and send up a few more prayers of thanksgiving in Notre Dame and Sacré-Coeur.

I know that not all cancer diagnoses have this type of ending. The people who inspire me as much as Natalie are her "cancer buddies" who are no longer here. I try to live my life and make decisions as if I were those individuals who are not here on earth.

# CHAPTER 8

# IDENTITY

*Hair Loss*

Your hair has never been better than it is when you are in your late teens. Let's face it, dragging a flat iron through partially wet hair and hearing that sizzle is somewhat satisfying. And somehow the finished product is always a ten! I laugh to myself, thinking back to the hairstyles that I rocked (did not rock) over the years. But when you're nineteen, your hair is your identity. It's what you make sure is just perfect before going out with your girls. You check yourself in the mirror several times before your date comes to pick you up. You have your friends fix your bangs before a photo is taken.

One of the first things I processed when I was diagnosed with cancer and they shared that the treatment plan would include chemotherapy was the fact that I would lose my hair. I heard "chemo" and instantly knew what that meant. Though, I'll admit, I was never bummed to see my hair go. I feel I am alone in this regard, as many women I know and love who have battled cancer have and continue to struggle with the loss of their locks. I didn't have the attachment to hair as all of my friends did in school. In fact, I remember telling a friend in high school, "I would go bald if I could...I am so *done* with doing my hair every day."

Although it was not something I cared much about losing, it still felt right to take time to process how losing my hair would make other people see me differently. In a way, I was grateful to lose it because at least people would know I was a fighter! It was my outward sign to other people that they could be strong too. The day I was to shave my head, I had a hair appointment with a hairdresser in downtown Charleston. In typical Charleston weather in September, we experienced a great flood that day, and the salon was shutting down before I could get to my appointment. I looked at my mother and told her, "I am mentally prepared to do this today. It has to be today." Since it was a normal recovery week for me out of the hospital, Dad was able to be back in Florence for a few days to get some work done. Mom and I were alone at the beach, and we were left to figure out the head-shaving technique.

My mother, the rock star, told me to get in the car and we'd go get an electric razor from Walmart. "We can do this ourselves!" she said. We picked out the top-shelf electric razor and headed back to the house. We laid down an old bedsheet, and my mother pulled one of our kitchen chairs onto the middle of the sheet. My mother's makeshift salon was complete with television and snacks. We were ready to rock in no time! I asked my mom if I could use scissors to cut the majority of the hair myself. I went to the bathroom so that I could watch myself go through the motions. I kept a basket in the sink where I took clump by clump in my fingers and snipped my beautiful long blond locks.

I decided to make light of the situation and gave myself many different hairstyles along the way that would set the stage for the full head shaving. I enjoyed the mullet stage, but it was short lived, for we had a job to do. My mom took the razor in her hands and began shaving. I recall her never hesitating. She's a badass. As I put my thoughts on paper from that day, I realize now how difficult that must have been for my own mother to take away the identity of her daughter. She did what was asked of her, not what was easy. I could have waited for a rescheduled appointment, but she knew the importance of grasping any bit of control that we could find, and this was a small piece.

We then moved back to the bathroom, where I sat in the shower, and my mother lathered my scalp with my dad's shaving cream. She was able to achieve a very close shave! I snapped photos along the way to send to my dad, Baxter, and Ragland. It was at the end that I realized what we had done. I was numb through the process, but as I felt the weightlessness of a bald head, I was shocked back into reality. I grabbed my head and felt my birthmark on my scalp that had always been covered up by my hair. I grabbed the hand mirror, and I turned to see the back side of my head to discover...damn! I have a pretty-shaped head!

I recall that the first few hours of being bald came with terrible headaches. The cold air shook me to my core as I tried to figure out how to manage the sensitivity my scalp was experiencing. All I could do was lie flat on the couch with a blanket on my head. I needed warmth since I had lost it all! I had a few scarves from friends and family that were given as gifts, but I struggled with texture on my bare scalp.

Choosing to be bald is not for the faint of heart. I recall friends coming to visit when I was first diagnosed, and they would squirm or frown when I talked about how I would lose my hair. I found that even though I was not upset about losing my hair, I began to change my perspective when people would see me for the first time bald and would frown in pity. I did my best to look past the sadness shown by others and decided to not be bothered by their shock. Losing my hair? Pshhh...I had a life to live! My main goal was to work on surviving.

After sending photos and getting rave reviews from family and friends, I told my mother I wanted to go out for dinner. I needed to own my new identity, and I knew the fastest way to do that was to jump right in. I posted a photo to Facebook that night so that everyone could see I was beating cancer to the punch. My caption was "Beating cancer to the punch! Bald and loving it!"

With Dad back in Florence for a few days and Baxter and Ragland back at school, my mother and I decided on one of our favorite restaurants, the Mustard Seed, which always had more locals than not under the roof. I knew this would be a safe space where I wouldn't feel all eyes on me the whole dinner. We walked in and sat down with our backs to the wall. We chatted about my new look and enjoyed our usual favorites. It almost felt like a normal night for us. I recall an older woman looking at me from across the restaurant. She continued to stare even when I purposefully made eye contact to let her know that she was staring. I realized she was waiting for me to acknowledge her. She followed with a smile to let me know that I looked good. I did look good! This stranger was the first of many "atta girls" that I would receive while bald. From women who had braved the bald head before me due to cancer treatment, to women who just admired, I enjoyed these looks and these smiles, for they reminded me of my own strength.

For all of the sweet smiles that came my way, I remember a few stares. After my four days of hibernation posttreatment, I told my dad I was really craving breakfast. He and I went to Isle of Palms to the Sea Biscuit, which is a restaurant notorious for having a wait. Dad went inside to give the hostess our name, and he told me to take a seat when one opened up. I snagged two seats on the bench on the front porch, which is similar to a packed elevator. People standing on top of each other looking like sardines. The sun was beating down on the front porch of Sea Biscuit, and it was nearly unbearable. I kept telling my dad I was fine to wait it out, but I could tell he was worried about me with the sun exposure. He grabbed a newspaper to shield my bald head from getting sun. When he did this, a boy around eight years old said out loud while staring at me, "I'm never getting cancer." His mother quickly reprimanded him and told him to hush. I knew what he meant. He was looking at me and trying to sympathize. He shared the only words he could after staring for several minutes. What he meant was that he never wants to go through what I was going through. If only saying it aloud was how it worked, kid.

I cannot even begin to comment on a struggle with feeling sexy or beautiful when bald because Ragland was the biggest hype man of all time. I've never felt as amazing as I did when I was bald and around him. Funny how you can mentally feel the strongest, but physically feel the weakest you've ever been.

Scarf or hat, bald or stubble, there's no right way to do it. Just do you.

*Mirror Struggles*

I remember as a little girl, I had a white wicker mirror that matched all of the white wicker furniture in my room. I used to put stickers all around the outer edge of the frame—specifically Lisa Frank and Volcom stickers. I had a wide appreciation for extracurricular activities as a child. I spent a lot of time in that mirror as a young girl practicing my dance moves or making funny hairdos. The freedom I felt to look like myself and embrace my figure at an age when many young girls begin to struggle with their image I consider a true blessing. I can thank my parents for always being the great encouragers and never, ever body shaming. I cannot recall a time when my mother mentioned needing to go on a diet or change something about the way she looked. Good on you, Mom!

This acceptance of my own body did not change as I grew older. I had great confidence in the way that I looked for many years leading up to my diagnosis. In fact, I remember wanting to pass my brother's marker on the scale in my parents' bathroom. I would give anything to be bigger than him! It's safe to say that nearly everything was a competition in the Hahn house.

After diagnosis, I spent time looking in the mirror, and whom I saw was not the person that I remembered precancer. No matter how hard I tried to force a smile, I could still see the look of fear deep inside. As treatment began, the deterioration process quickly set in. I experienced great discoloration. Pale ain't cute. In fact, I remember looking down at my hands while lying in my hospital bed, and I could practically see straight through my skin to the other side. It was as if I was simply a pile of flesh with no human element.

I would remain in the hospital for six days at a time per treatment cycle and was encouraged to walk the halls a few times each day to keep the blood flowing. I had a mirror and sink in my room, and when I would gain the strength to stand and walk the halls with my IV pole, I would pass by the mirror in the corner near the door. I hated that mirror. No matter how hard I tried to look away, I just couldn't. It was like a bad car wreck; you want to look away, but you just can't. I scared myself. The person I saw in the mirror was a ghost. She had no life to her, and sadness just radiated. I hated the way that I looked. But I often reminded myself, the worse I look, the harder the chemotherapy must be working. Ragland once compared the chemo to using mouthwash after brushing. Mouthwash burns when you use it, but it's a good kind of burn!

Small daily tasks like brushing my teeth came with a reminder of what I looked like. As I would be helped over to the sink to brush each morning and night, I spent a grueling two minutes (okay, not a full two minutes) watching a girl in the mirror I didn't know. Sunken-in cheeks and severe muscle loss were the makeup of the person in the mirror. It's fair to say I resembled Mr. Burns from *The Simpsons*.

During the days I spent at home recovering between my hospital stays, I relished in the stretch of good days I would experience where I could wear makeup and put on normal clothes. It's amazing what a little concealer can do to someone who is hurting so much inside. When I left the house to go on a date in high school, my mother would always say, "A little lipstick and that outfit will be perfect!" She was right. Adding just a bit of color to my face always made me smile back in the mirror. Those were the good days. Although short lived during a diagnosis, they were good.

*Join or Don't Join?*
Ovarian cancer is an interesting disease to have as a nineteen-year-old. When you battle a disease that typically affects women in their fifties and sixties, you feel alone. I remember researching local support groups for my type of cancer when I was

first diagnosed. I immediately quit trying when I read the description of one support group topic, which was something along the lines of helping women through the highs and lows of menopause. I may be one ovary down, but I'm not experiencing hot flashes.

Support groups are not for everyone. I laugh when I think back to my parents trying to get me in front of a therapist during treatment. I wanted nothing to do with sharing my feelings with someone who would pretend to understand or sympathize with me. My skewed view of what a therapist does was to my own detriment. Keeping to yourself and choosing to fight your own demons alone is not healthy or easy. I found myself in dark places that forced an unnecessary burden on me to be strong when it would have been better to share my thoughts and feelings with someone who was trained.

I chose not to join a support group during my treatment journey. It was my own personal decision at the time, and although I wish I could go back to help *prediagnosis me* cope, I needed to be in control of my own decisions. After finishing treatment and being on this side of survivorship, I have chosen to be an advocate for others to seek help during this stage of the journey.

*Music*

When I was a toddler, my family used to call me Baxterina. I am my dad's mini-me. I used to run around the house when I would see his car pulling in the driveway as he arrived home from work. I would anxiously wait for the clock to hit 5:30 p.m., and most evenings, I would hide under the church pew that was at our kitchen door so that I could grab his ankles and scare him as he walked inside. I remember being so excited for him to get home so that I could go in the garden with him and pick the vegetables that he worked so hard to grow. While in the garden, we would listen to the radio, which was always playing Motown hits. With each song, my dad would tell me the story behind the song lyrics. Our family jokes that Dad and I both know the manner in which many artists have died. What a weird piece of random knowledge to have stored in your brain. I cherish those days as a little girl in the garden with my dad and singing along to the Four Tops and the Isley Brothers. I believe this is where my cravings for music originated and helped me through many of my darkest days while living in the hospital, because music reminded me of a simpler time.

While in the hospital bed, I would plug in my headphones and listen to everything under the sun. With each song, I could feel a connection to the lyrics, which gave me a lifeline to the real world. In Ben Rector's song, "Hide Away," the lyrics "Sometimes I wanna follow Jesus, but sometimes He's hard to find" helped me on my down days. I needed the affirmation that when you know you are trying your hardest to find the good in a situation, sometimes it is just plain hard. I found myself praying so hard that my fists would hurt from how hard I would clench. It was as if the harder I prayed, the more likely it was that Jesus himself might appear in front of me and take away all of my pain. But no matter how hard I prayed some days, He was just hard to find.

As the chemotherapy began to drip, Earth, Wind, and Fire's "Fire" was always my song of choice because the medicine literally burned like fire. It was as if I had a theme song for each moment of my life. Christina Aguilera's "Fighter" was my anthem as I pushed through the final days of my inpatient regimen.

Stevie Wonder has always been a favorite of mine and my dad's. "For once in my life, I have someone who needs me, someone I've needed so long," I would sing as I would encounter the tough days, knowing I had family and Ragland who needed me to be strong. And let's not pretend that Gucci Mane and a few AC/DC hits didn't grace my playlist. I'm sure that visitors passing by my hall while I was sleeping would see a peaceful and quiet room. Little did they know that in my head I was practicing my song of choice for karaoke, "I Wanna Dance with Somebody."

Music is a beautiful thing, and it has and always will be a gift that I am grateful I can experience each day. For me, it was a bit of nostalgia and my constant comfort. And a reminder of the special bond that a dad and a daughter share.

## Afraid of Sleep

Each night during my cancer battle, I would become anxious as the sun went down. I remained calm on the exterior, but I felt a great sense of uneasiness in my heart as it neared time for me to get to bed. As I reflect on these thoughts on the other side of cancer, I realize that my uncertainty stemmed from the fears of what tomorrow would bring. I never knew how I would feel until I put my feet on the floor the next day, and it was bedtime that stood between me and my next obstacle. The toll that the treatments took on my body had me eager to rest, but I knew that sleep brought about the worries.

Silence can be the death of a cancer patient. My dad used to tell me that when I would remain silent in the hospital bed during treatment, he knew that was the sign that I was in great pain. My parents would come over to my bedside to check if I was still breathing. When you are in the hospital for treatment, there is no ceasing of alarms and monitors that are connected to your body. Patient care techs make their way to your room every few hours to check your vitals. There is no sleep in a hospital. Secretly, I liked it that way.

Not only was I fearful of bedtime, but I can recall lying in my bed and seeing the sun peek through the blinds in my bedroom and wishing I hadn't woken up. Not in a morbid way, but in an "I can't do this again" way. I was so tired of fighting from the day before, and the sun symbolized another day to get right up and do it all over again.

I would often muster up the strength to roll out of bed, only to put my feet on the floor and loudly proclaim, "Nope!" and slide back into bed. There were days that it was just *not* happening. And that was okay! I eventually realized and accepted the fact that I was allowed to move at my own pace, my new pace. My cancer pace.

# CHAPTER 9
# DEATH

My first real experience with death was when I was five. I remember my paternal great-grandmother's funeral in Hendersonville, North Carolina. Our family was positioned in the front pew right in front of the casket. I remember the church being full of people, and I remember my grandmother, Sue Sue, being very calm as she laid her mother to rest. She's always been quite stoic. We used to laugh that she didn't know what a rearview mirror was because she ripped it off when she got in the car. She never has been one to look back. I admire a woman like that. Before the funeral, we had the traditional visitation in the church hall. I was unable to see inside the open casket from where I stood, but I remember trying to peek in. Sue Sue saw me struggling and came over to pick me up. As I sat on her hip, she told me about where Mimi had gone and that she was now resting peacefully. As any curious five-year-old would, I asked Sue Sue what the brown bump was on Mimi's chin. She told me it was her mole. "You want to touch it?" she asked me. "Yes," I said, and I touched my deceased great-grandmother's mole.

It wasn't until a few years later that my maternal great-grandmother passed away. Mama was wicked smart and died just twenty-three days shy of her 105th birthday. When we would visit Mama at her nursing home, she would recite Shakespeare and not miss a line. She was as sharp as a tack. The funeral was certainly a celebration of life. Living such a long life and seeing so much must have been exhausting.

I was older for Mama's funeral, and I remember the sadness in the church. It was hard to watch my family mourn, and I recall thinking if we were all this sad for a nearly 105-year-old passing away, I could not imagine the pain my friends felt as they buried their grandparents who would be nearly thirty years younger. Or even my friends who would later bury parents when we got to middle school. It was at Mama's funeral that I realized the pain isn't any easier the older a person is when they pass. I would later learn that when you bury a friend, the pain can be unimaginable.

## Survivor's Guilt

I was sent home from the hospital after unhooking from my IV pole for the last time. Baxter and Ragland were both on their way home from college for the weekend to celebrate me crossing the finish line with treatment. We would still anxiously await the final numbers three weeks later, but I was told that my team of doctors were confident that with my low counts heading into my final treatment, we could begin the celebrations.

I was lying on the couch, waiting for the boys to walk through the door, when my left arm began to swell like Popeye. I called my mom from the kitchen and showed her the redness and heaviness that had taken over my bicep. She called my grandmother, Nonnie, who is a retired nurse and knows it all. Nonnie said, "Get in the car, and get to the ER." I knew in my heart that something was wrong, but I didn't want to believe it. It was supposed to be my downtime with the guys to celebrate no more needles and no more chemo! Dad was pulling in to town from Florence that evening for the celebrations, but his car barely stopped moving. Dad and I were off to the ER.

When we arrived, we were rushed back to room 1. As we waited for a nurse to come and give us our plan of action, I told my dad that all I wanted to do was to have some tests run and then head home. After all, my mother was making Mexican lasagna, and I couldn't let that go to waste. I was asked to move from the ER bed to a wheelchair so that they could do an ultrasound on my arm. The quiet technician pushed me through the empty halls of the x-ray floor (I'm certain there's a more technical term). The ultrasound tech was revving up the computer as she instructed me on which way to lay my arm. As she was telling me the gel would be cold, I remember thinking how we needed to get this show on the road so I could get home.

Her fluid motions on one spot led me to believe something wasn't right. She hovered over the middle of my armpit and sighed. "You've got a big clot right there. Yep. There it is." I said, "Blood clot?" A few more clicks of her pointer, and she had me on my way back down to the ER. The transport tech and I remained quiet the whole way down the elevator. I silently cried as my control slipped through my fingers. Here we go again.

My dad was sitting in room 1 as I was wheeled back in, and I burst into tears. All I could muster up were the words "I don't get to go home! I have to spend the night in this stupid place again!" The moment you think you are regaining control of the life that was once spiraling out of control, you are thrown right back on the ride. This is cancer.

I was admitted back to 7 West, the same hall, in my usual bed with my usual nurses. As I was wheeled down to my room, we passed by the nurses' station, where my eyes met the charge nurse's. She saw me as she was typing on the computer, and she dropped her face into her hands and began shaking her head. This kind soul had seen me through so much, and she knew I was disheartened that I was being forced to take steps backward. I was so angry, and my frustration was misdirected at the people who were just trying to help. But for the life of me, I couldn't understand why God had me back in this place just as I was preparing to celebrate. I remained on 7 West for the weekend until they could get my white counts in order. That Sunday, I was told I could be discharged after about an hour of paperwork that my care team needed to complete. My mom went down the hall to gather something from the nurses' station and passed by a room with another young girl in the bed. The name on her door was the same as my doctor.

My mom came back to the room to share what she had seen and encouraged me to go down the hall to introduce myself. "Surely she is in for something similar to you! She's lost her hair, too, and could probably use a friend." My mom and I walked down the hall to my soon-to-be new friend's room and knocked on the door. I met one of my very best friends that day. Her name was Kendra.

Over the next three years, Kendra and I would celebrate through remissions and recurrences, setbacks and good news. All through it, we were the only young ones with this disease that we knew. We clung to each other for answers and would text about which hall was best for riding your IV pole like a scooter. When I went back to Wofford for my spring semester of college, Kendra was still back on 7 West fighting her battle. I struggled with why I was able to move on with life and my friend was stuck. She was stuck in our hall, attached to her IV pole. I was walking outside, and she was walking the halls of the hospital. I still don't have answers for why I am here and she's not.

She passed away after three years of an incredible fight. As I sat in the pew of her memorial service, I recalled my sadness from every other funeral I had been to in my life. Why did this one hurt a different hurt? This one stung from such a deep place. The two pews in front of us were filled with the doctors, nurses, and patient-care technicians who took care of her. They were hurting too. This pain was different from losing a great-grandmother or a friend's parent. Losing a fellow fighter means losing hope. In this moment, I learned what it meant to have survivor's guilt.

I struggled with accepting the fact that my cards were different from hers. I always wondered why I got to move forward with life and Kendra's was taken. I still wonder. I've learned to move through those thoughts by choosing to be an advocate for those still battling the disease. Let's be honest: the battle never ends.

*Cemeteries*

Cemeteries. A morbid thing to talk about in a book that's supposed to be about hope and finding positivity. But where I grew up, you pass cemeteries on back roads like you pass Dollar Generals. They are everywhere, and they have old and new headstones. Most times you will see a funeral home tent erected in the middle of the cemetery, either in preparation for a service or being taken down. There's usually fresh dirt from a recent burial and many flowers. Sometimes, you'll see a family adding new flowers to a burial plot. You may even see my crazy extended family singing Christmas carols to our deceased relatives during the holidays. This statement really deserves its own chapter.

I started to see cemeteries differently when I was diagnosed, as I began to feel as though I was cheating death each day. As my dad and I traveled the back roads from our home in Florence for me to receive treatment the next day in Charleston, we passed an old cemetery. As we listened to music and cruised the bumpy roads, I asked my dad where he wanted to be buried. He shared with me his wishes and then paused for a bit. He asked, "Is that something you've been thinking about?" I hadn't realized that's where my mind was going, but it was. I had been thinking about where I might like to rest after all of this was over. If I didn't receive favorable results or if the doctors would share with me that there was nothing else they could do, I had better start thinking about those details myself.

My eyes began to well up with tears as I responded to my dad where I'd like to be buried. I told him I wanted to be cremated and scattered in the ocean. "That's my happy place." I cry thinking about how that question made my dad feel. I wonder what he felt as a father knowing his daughter's mind was in such a dark place. There was nothing he could do to change those thoughts. Mentally, that's the place I was in, and my headspace was often filled with dark thoughts.

# CHAPTER 10
# EYE OF THE STORM

Having grown up in South Carolina, I know a bit about hurricanes. Whether we were evacuating from them or praying that they turned east, I always remember hearing stories of family and friends who chose to stay during Hurricane Hugo in 1989. It was a hurricane that registered as a category 4, but those who lived to tell the tale really would prefer to give the storm the proper credit of being labeled a category 5.

I had a friend tell me that she and her family went outside during the storm just as the eye passed over the coast. It was as if they were experiencing a normal, sunny day, and the wind had slowed. A few minutes were granted to those in the path of the storm to step outside and assess the damage, regroup, and head back in for shelter. In many ways, I can reference a few times that I felt like I was in the eye of the storm during my cancer journey.

Trips up to Wofford during the days that my numbers were strong and allowed me to be in public were perfect examples of being in the eye of the storm. I stood with my ZTA sisters during Bid Day and had energy that I had not had days before. Ragland and I attended a KA Halloween party as Dr. Evil and Mini-Me.

On days where I felt well enough to venture out for a lunch date or to visit friends, I remember thinking that this must be what the eye of a storm feels like. As you move throughout your day and you feel as though you have some slice of normalcy, you are quickly reminded of the new normal that you live and that life will soon shock you back to cancer reality. On these days, I prayed for the good feelings to last. I so badly wanted to ride the wave of feeling like my normal self. I knew it wouldn't last long, but I loved those moments where the fog had lifted and my vision had cleared.

*Pots and Pans*

The common phrase "stop and smell the roses" is not always applicable to cancer patients. You don't want to stop and smell anything when you are nauseous morning, noon, and night. In fact, the smells that you once loved become the very scents that have you hurling on the side of the road next to your favorite burger stop.

And so I prefer the phrase "stop to hear pots and pans." After my first treatment and the initial wave of nausea and vomiting, I took a golf cart ride with my friend, now sister-in-law, Suiter. It was one of my first outings with no hair. Truly, it was pure bliss, as I finally had the strength to venture outside and feel the wind in my hair (scalp). Being able to breathe and not immediately dry heave from smells made me feel like myself.

We passed by an old home on the island, and from the open window, I could hear people in the kitchen. They were "piddling," as my dad would say, and washing dishes in the sink. The clinging and clanging of the pots and pans were familiar sounds, yet I had never "heard" them before. My life before cancer was always busy. Rushing from one activity to the next, thriving on a full calendar. I slept hard every night, knowing that I put 100 percent into each day. But, for the first time, I heard simplicity. I heard a family in the kitchen of an old home on Sullivan's Island washing dishes after a meal together. It was a beautiful sound. People were taking time to spend with one another and performing what most would consider a mundane task. But, through the eyes and ears of a cancer patient, it was people living.

I shared this story with my family later in my treatment when we were discussing what a cancer journey is like. As much as you may try, you can never quite depict what it's like to have cancer because each day is a new experience. The world around you doesn't stop. That may be one of the most painful things to face each day. It's a Friday night, and your friends are headed to a fraternity function. You look out your hospital window to see a stranger lacing up their tennis shoes to go for a run. You say goodbye to your day-shift nurse who is going home to be with her family. You? You're doing the furthest thing from that. You remain in the hospital bed in a gown worn by at least fifty other people, listening to the beeping of your IV pole.

I told them that cancer is hell. But cancer gives you something that not everyone in this world is privileged to experience. It gives you the view to see life in its pure beauty. It shows you the simple things you once took for granted. Cancer points you to the things that bring you happiness in life. Cancer can take a lot of things from you, but it will never shield you from seeing or hearing the beauty this life has to offer. If you take time to sit back and breathe, just listen. You will hear the pots and pans.

*White Feathers*

The day before my doctor's appointment for my annual physical, I was driving back roads along the coast of South Carolina. I was leaving Ragland's family's beach house and heading home to Charleston for the night for my quick doctor's appointment. Before I left that afternoon, we watched the Weather Channel, as there was a severe storm running the coast. I decided to make a break for it and try to beat the storm, but

I ended up tackling it head-on. I drove through some of the worst rain I had ever experienced, only to find a thick layer of fog on the other side. After twenty minutes of a complete downpour, I called Ragland to let him know I made it through to clear skies. The skies were not clear, but the rain had stopped. There was a blanket of fog that covered the road, and I could barely see a few yards in front of me. The lights on my car were of no help, so I blindly followed the white lines and told Ragland I was just going to back off my speed to be on the safe side.

There were no other cars around me. It was an open road covered with thick fog. The only way I could describe the experience was that it was as if someone had dropped a sheet on my car. "Everything is white!" I told Ragland. In order to focus, I turned my radio down and drove in silence. I remember the odd peace that I experienced alone on the road as I made my way south to Charleston and eventually made it home to sunny skies.

Throughout my cancer journey, I would find white feathers all over the place. I enjoyed covering myself in down comforters and figured that was the reason for the feathers that I would find in peculiar places. It was not until later that when a friend asked me to describe my experience with cancer in one word that I would say the word "white." I told her, "I don't know why, but I feel like I am constantly in a state of white noise. Everything around me is softened. Noises are softened, my vision is softened, and my emotions are softened. All I can say is that the color white is the best way to describe my state of being at this moment."

Angel wings have always been of interest to me. I love how intricate they are, and each one is different than the next. As a little girl, I told people I had a guardian angel named Rosie. My grandmother Nonnie has a guardian angel whom she named Rose. As my grandmother's namesake, I felt it was fitting to name my angel Rosie. My grandmother taught me to thank Rosie when we found a parking spot close to the grocery store. Or, when I would lose something and find it, she would say, "Thank you, Rose!" I believe these beautiful white feathers that I found along the way were from angels' wings. These were soft reminders that I was being carried through this journey. My favorite verse quickly became Psalm 91 (NIV):

> He who dwells in the shelter of the Most High will rest in the shadow of the Almighty. I will say of the Lord, "He is my refuge and my fortress, my God, in whom I trust. Surely He will save you from the fowler's snare and from the deadly pestilence. He will cover you with His feathers, and under His wings you will find refuge."

What could be more white and pure than feathers from an angel? Surely, this served as the greatest comfort and remained my constant source of security during the fight of my life. My God and angel army were with me. Always.

# CHAPTER 11
# HOSPITAL STAYS

For someone who had never stayed the night in a hospital before, I was forced to quickly welcome the halls of 7 West as my new home in short order. If you've never stayed the night at a hospital before, consider yourself fortunate. The best way to describe the hospital at night to those who have not experienced it would be to compare it to my freshman dorm. When I would have to pee in the middle of the night, I would wander out of my room and head to the hall bathroom. The walls were white and completely silent, which was the exact opposite of just twelve hours earlier.

I heard someone once say that the loneliest they were while sick with cancer was in the middle of the night during their hospital stays. No one gets sleep in a hospital, but instead you receive your treatment and lie wide awake, processing each beep that comes from your IV pole. You do not need an alarm clock because the truth is, you never actually went to sleep. REM cycles are BS when you are a patient in the hospital. It's about as foreign as clean sheets.

When I think about those lonely moments I experienced while lying in the hospital bed, I think that it must be a similar feeling to those who are in jail. An *incanceration*, if you will. When you wake up, you'll have to face the same obstacles from the day prior, and there's not much hope in sight. In fact, some days, you don't want to wake up.

As I process those days now that I am on the other side, I recall the generous individuals who took time out of their days to volunteer and be with others who were struggling. This one guy used to come around each Saturday on his day off and would play guitar for those who were admitted on 7 West. He would strum along and sing to me. The fact that he would take the time to spend his day out of the office with those who were so sick always touched me. This was one of those moments when I realized that some people need the blessing of just knowing they are giving back. As wonderful as it was to have someone play guitar, I always thought he needed that more than me.

Aside from the loneliness, you are gifted extremely knowledgeable individuals who are there to serve you. I would like to believe that there is a special place in heaven for people in health care. As we see the doctors and nurses head home, we assume they are going back to their families to live a normal life. What I know to be true is that's not the case. These individuals are remembering their patients in the hospital and the struggles that we are facing. They don't forget about us.

### Life Hacks in the Hospital

If you are reading this as a non-cancer-survivor, you should know it is imperative that before you go into the hospital for any procedure, you should always consult your closest cancer friend about the dos and don'ts to hospital stays. We know every cheat code, and honestly, there could be an entire book just on that. But instead of writing about insurance and which stool softener is the best, I figured it would be more enjoyable for all parties reading this to talk about the mental life hacks of being a patient in the hospital.

*Hospital Hack 1: Hospital Decor*

Each time I checked in for another round of chemotherapy, my family would decorate my hospital room to reflect a specific theme. No white walls were allowed, as we all believed it was important to surround yourself with things most familiar and comforting. The following themes graced my hospital room: White Feathers, Wizard of Oz, Margaritaville, and Princess. I'm sure all of the other patients just assumed I went a little heavy on the Ativan when they would peek in my room. I was blessed, and still am, to have such wonderful family and friends who would aid in the rearranging of the bland hospital decor to provide a fun and relaxing place for me to heal. I believe that was the first time the floor had ever heard a blender churning food, other than when they were needed to make smoothies for the "nonsolids" patients.

*Hospital Hack 2: Observe the Healthy*

A post-surg floor is often a place of respite (for patients, never nurses), where you typically only hear the beeping from an IV pole signaling a kink in the line or a completion of fluids. There is not much life to be found on the floor of a hospital handling patients in this state. As I would take one of my three daily walks down the hall, I found it important to take in as much happening on the hall as I could. Being confined to your room and not seeing much action was always good motivation to get up and walk, even when I felt my worst. I would mosey on over toward the window that overlooked Charleston, and I would watch people going about their days. As difficult as it was for me to watch, it was great inspiration for me to get back to that place one day.

*Hospital Hack 3: Say Your Prayers*

On the days where I was angry at everyone and felt like there was no way out, I would pray. I stayed quiet in my hospital bed and tried to focus my aggression toward something productive, like praying. I find that my prayers when I'm angry are often harsh. "Lord, I am begging you to please let me get some rest." "Lord, please make the pain stop because I cannot take another second." "Lord, do not do this to me." I would take a few moments to breathe and reflect on what I really wanted to pray for rather than what my emotions were telling me to pray for. I channeled my anger into thought and came away with more productive prayers. They then turned to "Lord, I pray that I can find the peace to rest." "Lord, please help me to remember to remain calm in these difficult and painful moments." "Lord, let Your will be done." My heart would be lighter after I changed my focus. Quiet time followed by honest prayer was the greatest hospital hack.

# CHAPTER 12
# THE "WTF" MOMENTS

There were a lot of these. (Better known as "WTHeck moments" when your grandmother is reading.) Moments where I thought I had everything under control and then, like the flip of a switch, my life would change. "Where has my life gone?" I would ask myself. I had a picture-perfect childhood, protected and surrounded by the people who loved me the most. Fear and anxiety only plagued me as I grew older, and that was because it was in my genes. But I never worried about surviving. All you do is worry about surviving when you are faced with cancer.

Time spent in the hospital can easily be categorized as a "WTF moment." On your elevator ride up to the hospital floor for your six-day stay, you pass healthy people coming and going as they visit family and friends. They all have visitor badges for their short hour-long stay. Meanwhile, you have your red bandage wrapped around your arm from the blood draw earlier that morning, which just sets the stage for the port accessing and multiple other IVs awaiting your arrival. WTF is happening? When did your life change so quickly from picture perfect and healthy to ill and fragile?

One of my most vivid WTF moments was right after my third treatment. I could hardly breathe after I received my Neulasta injection. For those who have never received Neulasta, just imagine your bones growing and growing, but your skin not stretching. Your joints are on fire, and it's the worst case of the flu you've experienced. Lather on some serious postchemo nausea, and there you have it. After the injection, I collapsed on the floor of the infusion suite. I looked up at my mom, who was kneeling down to help me up off the floor. I had no muscles in my legs, and I remember wanting to cry but having no strength to do so. The sweet nurse who administered the injection ran back into the room and handed me a green bag (barf bags for those fortunate enough to not be familiar with them). I vomited with so much force that I had nothing left after several minutes. I was screaming with each heave, as the pain was just unbearable.

I said out loud, "Please pass out, please pass out!" If I could just faint, I would be unconscious and wouldn't have to face the pain. The nurse told my mother that she needed to get me to the ER quickly and that she could call an ambulance, but it may take more time for them to reach us in the infusion suite than it would take for my mom to wheel me over. My mom decided to throw me in the wheelchair and run me the two hundred yards to the ER. Along that hot sidewalk, the foot pedals on the wheelchair gave way, and the tops of my bare feet shredded on the sidewalk. The wheels kept getting stuck in the jagged pavement, and with each bump, I would whimper.

This. This was a WTF moment. Heaving, sweating, scratched, and broken. How did my life get so bad, so fast? As we made our way to the air-conditioned ER waiting room, it was apparent that I would be better off locked in the bathroom due to my low white blood cell count. My mother locked me in the hall bathroom until I was called back so that I wouldn't contract the thousand other diseases that crawled the walls of the ER.

After two bags of fluid and plenty of antinausea medicine, I was sent on my way. And just like that, in the car on the way home from the ER, I looked out the window, and all I could say was "WTF."

There are better WTF moments that happen during a cancer journey. Ones that, believe it or not, are filled with hope and excitement. My favorite of these was on the day that I was told there was no evidence of disease. My parents were asked to step out while my gynecological oncologist came into the room to perform my usual pelvic exam. While they were out in the hallway, the doctor walked into my room with the biggest smile. She said, "You're done!" with open arms. I screamed "What?" in disbelief, as I could not believe I had made it. I began to hold back tears, as business was business, and she quickly went into the pelvic exam portion. Crying and pelvic exams don't go well together. My parents heard me crying and tried to walk back into the exam room, but I yelled at them to keep the door shut. All modesty goes out the window when you have cancer, but I didn't need the whole hall to see my hoo-hah.

After the pelvic exam was finished, the doctor left me to change and said she would be back in to discuss the details of the blood work and what I should expect moving forward. I sat on the table for a few moments all alone. I treasure that time so much, as it gave me a moment to just thank God. I've always wondered about my friends and family who have had real conversations with God, and I have secretly wished I could have one of those myself. All my life, I've craved to hear actual words from God. This day I realized that I didn't have to hear the exact words to know that God was speaking to me. It was just God and me in that exam room, and the only words that I could muster were "Thank you, God. Thank you." I felt Him respond in a way that I cannot describe, but the joy in my heart and the peace that I felt was the greatest feeling I've ever experienced.

I opened the door to my parents in the hallway, who were crying. All I could say was "I'm done."

It was done. The race was done. We all embraced, and we gathered back in the exam room to meet with the doctor. As she entered the room again, "Thank you" just didn't seem like the appropriate gesture of appreciation. I told her that I was so grateful for the care that she provided me and my entire family during this journey, and she began to cry. Here was another WTF moment. How in the world did we get to this point? We made it. This was the greatest WTF of all!

# CHAPTER 13
# THE STRENGTH OF LOVE

Ragland. I'm not sure there's a better person in this world than him. I knew the moment that I saw him in our upstairs playroom when he was hanging out with Baxter that I wanted him in my life and me in his. This was not to be easily mistaken by a normal crush of a thirteen-year-old girl. In fact, I think back to what I wore that day (rather, he reminds me often). "The puke-green headband" seemed like the perfect choice for my outfit that morning before I headed out the door for another day of eighth grade. Maybe if I had processed that I would be meeting my future husband for the first time, I would have left with a better hairdo. But, if I'm being honest, I needed more help during that phase in my life than just a different headband.

Baby-pink-colored braces and puke-green headband with my too-short bob were clearly what roped him in. I arrived home from volleyball practice and ran upstairs to the playroom, where I knew they were. I had heard Ragland's name from Baxter but hadn't had the chance to meet him. As I walked in the playroom and he introduced himself, I panicked and told him my name was Gertrude. I cringe typing that.

Ragland and I have been through quite a bit together. If he could love me through that eighth grade phase, he could love me through just about anything. Over the next year, we grew to be fast friends (in my eyes) as I palled around with my older brother and his best friend. Hell, I even learned to skim board for him. Ragland went off to boarding school for ninth grade, which was seven hours away, and I lost all hope of landing a shot with him. I laugh (read: cry), thinking to myself how confident I was, and you'd understand what I mean if you compared my yearbook photo to his yearbook photo. We kept in touch over the first year he was away at school, and I watched myself rise and fall on his MySpace Top 8. I always felt like I missed my shot, but was grateful even to just call him my friend our freshman year of high school.

We would text back and forth on our Blackberrys, and I would pretend my phone accidentally deleted my messages so that I could text him and say, "Did you text me? I thought I saw your name pop up, but my phone just deleted all of my messages—ugh!" His response was often "No," but it always segued nicely to the start of a long conversation. And that, ladies, is how it's done!

Two years passed, and we still remained great friends. I considered him my best friend and always wished that he would make the move, and one day he did. He asked me up for a big weekend at his school and offered for me to bring a friend. "I mean, if you want!" I immediately called my friend, who I knew would be up for it, and she agreed. A few days later, my friend ended up backing out due to a conflict, and I was set to ride seven hours in the car with his mother to the boarding school.

We still laugh about our seven-hour car ride with no radio. We chatted the whole way about all things under the sun. I cherish that car ride so very much. My heart was happy and joyful because I was finally on my way to be with Ragland, and as we both knew, we were always more than friends.

Three days and a Facebook official status later, we began dating. We dated the rest of high school and found ourselves looking at some of the same colleges. I wanted big; he wanted small. He committed to Wofford College in December, early action. I knew in my heart that after two years of long-distance dating, it was time to be together. But I also knew my desire for independence and that we had already mastered seven hours. What was two or three?

After a deposit was in the envelope to Georgia, I pulled back. In my heart, I was pushing Wofford away because I didn't want to be the girl who followed the boy. But it was where I belonged. As much as I wanted to believe I needed a big school, I knew where I would truly thrive. I decided on Wofford that following April, and we were both bound for the same campus. We loved each other through all of the struggles of freshman year. I joined a sorority, and he joined a fraternity, all while being true to each other and keeping our promise to love one another and try to make it work. He went along with each sorority function costume I forced him to wear, and I slept in the woods and peed behind cars in forty-degree weather at Mountain Weekend.

We were finally making memories together, and I was just grateful to be so close. But the summer of 2012 was a true test of our love. You do not know the weight of someone's love until you depend on it to get up each day. I've never been able to comprehend the love that Ragland gives me. Constant, steadfast, unshaken love. To share the news with a nineteen-year-old guy that his girlfriend has been struck with a life-altering illness, you expect anger. You expect fear. Of course, sadness. But Ragland's acceptance of the diagnosis is a perfect example of the strong man that he is.

My mom recalled the feelings she experienced when she looked at Ragland in the waiting room as the doctor shared the news of the severity of the disease. She could see his mind racing internally, but his extremely calm demeanor showed on the outside. This is my Ragland. Always thinking of ways to fix situations, but remaining strong for others.

Ragland proposed on December 30, 2017, in the sweetest way I could have imagined. When I was facing my fourth chemotherapy treatment and staying in the hospital, Ragland drove in from Wofford for the night to surprise me. That hospital stay was princess themed, and my prince showed up in his best-looking suit with a glass slipper on a pillow. Five years after his sweet gesture, his family was in town, and we were all staying at my parents' house after a concert downtown the night before. Before I fell asleep that Friday night, Ragland bet me fifty dollars I couldn't sleep past 8:00 a.m. I needed the money, so I agreed to the bet, not even thinking twice about his odd request. Now that I type this, I realize just how gullible this sounds.

At 7:00 a.m. the next morning, Ragland showed up in his same suit from the hospital with the same pillow that held the slipper. Instead of the slipper, a Croghan's ring box was perched on top. He clicked on the lamp on my bedside table, and I jolted up and asked if he had to go to work that day. He got down on one knee and shared the sweetest words. I cried so hard, but was just grateful I didn't wear my retainer to bed that night. I had drool on my face, and my hair looked a mess. I smile still thinking back to that morning and the joy I felt in my heart, which is the same joy I feel each day knowing he is mine and I am his.

My journey became our journey. When we said our vows on our wedding day, "through sickness and in health" packed more meaning than most wedding ceremonies. We had already loved each other through sickness. We had seen such dark times together, and we landed on our feet. He was walking beside me and holding me up when I felt I could not stand any longer. He is the best person I've ever known, and I can't imagine the journey through cancer without him.

I write this chapter because love was such a huge component of my healing. I'm grateful to God for creating a crossing of our paths. My middle school crush became my high school sweetheart, who became my teammate, who became my husband. Cancer weakens so many things in your life. But not our love for each other. It never could.

## CHAPTER 14
# LIFE AFTER CANCER

The moment the doctor shares with you that you are finished with treatment, you gain an incredible sense of freedom. But you embark on a journey that is completely foreign and intimidating. I believe the medical world fails us cancer survivors in this department, as they work so diligently to get us healthy, but they abandon us after proclaiming, "You're free!"

Similar to a boat being pushed away from the dock and floating out in the water, cancer survivors can often relate to this freedom. It's a welcomed honor to no longer have to call your doctor each week with new and never-before-experienced symptoms. Don't get me wrong! It's wonderful to cut the umbilical cord. But there's certainly a source of comfort on the floors of a hospital that's hard to understand until you find yourself no longer wearing an inpatient bracelet.

I wish I had a manual to help all cancer patients navigate the waters, but it's a path that must be cleared by the individual, and not just by referencing a generic map. For me, it took time and patience to understand how much my body had changed and transformed during those months of treatment. Realizing that it wasn't feasible to jump back into the swing of things was a difficult pill to swallow. There is a physical, emotional, and mental recovery that must take place. I wanted so badly to live the life I had prior to the disease, but as any cancer survivor will tell you, your life after treatment is so much richer than it was before diagnosis.

The level of appreciation for each day that we wake up is something that I wish everyone could understand. Those of us fortunate to walk this path have the beauty of knowing this feeling each day that we rise out of bed. It's a joy that is rewarded to those who have fought the good fight, and it's the greatest medal that I've ever worn.

*Rearview-Mirror Moments*

After receiving amazing news that there is no evidence of disease, it's common to have an identity crisis. You've been living a life of fear and confusion for the last few months, and you wonder what the next few will hold. I even found myself missing my diagnosis because at least I knew who I was during those months...the girl with cancer.

For days after my final appointment where I received the all-clear, I wondered what my new normal would be like and how I would handle getting back to the normal day-to-day. I struggled more than I care to admit. I suffered from depression and anxiety, where I found myself questioning each and every pain that I encountered. I returned back to Wofford for my second semester of my sophomore year, only to be reminded of my disease each day.

I would leave friends' dorms to run back to my room and grab my blood-thinning shots. I administered one hundred of these bad boys over the course of three months following the blood clot in my arm. While my friends were deciding which boots to wear out and curling their hair, I was busy searching for an alcohol swab in my top drawer so I could sterilize my skin before giving myself the injection.

My favorite times for reflection were in the early mornings. I found myself craving the quietness of the dorm at these hours because it reminded me of a place that I knew well…the hospital halls. I would force myself to get up around 7:00 a.m., even on the weekends, so that I could find a bit of solace. How odd it must have seemed for those who were on the outside looking in that someone who lived such a difficult few months was yearning to go back to that time. I remember feeling that I needed a new identity when I was no longer deemed "sick" by medical standards. Schoolwork seemed so lame to me, and the worries that my peers had just seemed to carry no weight in my mind. I would roll my eyes at the trivial matters that seemed to weigh heavily on friends. I was becoming difficult to be around and a person I didn't want to be.

These were rearview-mirror moments of mine. I couldn't help but continue to think back to what I had just experienced and how I needed/wanted/prayed to be back in the safe space again. It was a strange request to want that lifestyle again, but it was something I grew to know and love. I missed my doctors and my nurses; I missed my parents and my dogs. I missed my bald head. I missed the beeping from the blasted IV pole.

I was not in a good place, and I realized it soon after returning to school. I knew that I needed to make a choice to move on and, of course, never forget the obstacles I faced, but that God needed me to be present in this chapter of my life. I knew that was where I should be, and I had to trust my faith that I would soon gain the strength to accept it.

### The Need to Relate

Walking through a crowd and spotting someone with a bald head is so exhilarating to me. I don't mean to downplay the severity of having no hair and what that means, but I find myself enjoying chatting with people who are currently going through cancer treatment. It's a "need to relate" that I have felt since I finished chemotherapy and the desire to help in some way.

When I was going through treatment, people came out of the woodwork to share with me their stories of their battle with cancer. I am now that person. I love to share my story and be as transparent as I can with others because I know people are curious. People would always ask, "How did you find it?" and immediately follow the questions with "I have a daughter your age." When adults see young people struggling, they quickly think of the closest person to them that is similar in age. They want to sympathize with you and let you know how sorry they are for your situation. Without fail, you'll find many frowns those first few days of sporting your bald head. Little do people realize that being bald is badass and empowering.

Now, whenever I see someone who is bald and it's clear that they are undergoing treatment, I always go out of my way to tell them how awesome they look and how great it is that they are freely going bald.

*Careful What Ya Say*

Good gosh. *People.* Quit saying, "Sorry!" You aren't sorry. You are sad, but you aren't sorry. You are not the reason that I had cancer. You apologize to someone when you've done something wrong, not when you are sad. *Sorry* is such a pitiful word. I would tell people who would share how sorry they were that I didn't need the pity. Instead, tell me that you are thinking of me and praying for better days. Give action to the pity! Let me know that you really do care. And, please, do not tell me about the time your friend's grandmother had the same cancer and she turned out just fine. No diagnosis is the same. Never compare.

One of the greatest gestures I experienced from friends and family during my journey was the unexpected cards and text messages. I gained strength from the encouragement given to me by my peers. I realize "I'm sorry" is a natural reaction to sadness. When someone passes away, we share with the loved ones of the deceased that we are "so sorry" for their loss. Sometimes, "sorry" is the only word that comes to mind. I challenge you to speak slowly and give more thought to your condolences. Here's a cheat sheet for all of you who need a little help:

"I was so very sad to hear of your diagnosis, but I am praying for you, and my prayers include _____."

"You are going to fight this, and we are beside you each step of the way."

"How can I help? Would you like for a friend to join you at your next infusion?"

"I have an open morning this week and need to run to the grocery store. Send me your list!"

"I love you."

# CHAPTER 15
# LEARNING TO OPENLY THANK GOD

Growing up in a Catholic family, I used to beg my mom to let my brother and me go to the Presbyterian youth group. The Presbyterian church was just down the street from our house, and all of the other neighborhood kids would attend on Wednesday nights. "They play basketball!" we would argue. You couldn't get much more opposite than our CCD (Confraternity of Christian Doctrine) classes. We sat in classrooms for one whole hour on Wednesday nights and had to make our way through workbooks. They also conveniently squeezed in opportunities for confession in the church. Confession or basket-ball? That's a no-brainer for a fifth grader.

In high school, I would have conversations with friends about their youth groups and which book they were studying in the Bible. My friends could rattle off their favorite verses like there was nothing to it. Catholics don't claim to know specific Bible verses, so I found myself keeping quiet during these conversations. It wasn't something I felt confident contributing to, so I chose to sit back and listen.

I have always felt that I had a strong faith, but one that was not comfortable being outward facing. My parents are both devout Christians, and my grandparents attend daily Mass. I'm so thankful for the Christian foundation they have raised us on, but I still always felt like I was missing a key component of my own faith. I knew I needed to experience a connection with the Lord on my own and it would come in due time.

When you're faced with a life-threatening illness, many people choose to cling to a higher power. After you survive being dragged through the trenches, it's hard *not* to believe that there is a

God. But when you watch beautiful people leave this world so young, it can be a struggle to remember that God is always good. Our priest growing up opened each Mass the same way:

PRIEST: "God is good."
CONGREGATION: "All the time."
PRIEST: "All the time."
CONGREGATION: "God is good!"

I always enjoyed this part of the Mass. It served as a beautiful reminder that yes, God *is* good. In all things, we must honor Him.

Throughout my cancer journey, I met bitter and frustrated people who lingered long in the "Why me?" stage. I cannot imagine the pain and the anger that these individuals carried every day. I hurt knowing that others failed to have the hope for a greater being who served as their Shepherd. My heart was light because I knew that I was loved by God. This diagnosis was not a punishment or karma for my actions in life. This was an opportunity that was intended to be viewed as a gift. I prayed to God each night that I would be healed and that I would one day know the reason for this gift.

I think we often get caught up in the thought that if someone isn't healed from their cancer, this is God failing. I believe that this is simply the devil giving his best attempt at driving us further from our faith. I do not know why people die from cancer after years of fighting. I'm unsure why young women battle cancer with tough chemotherapy regimens to hopefully, one day, bear children, and the end result is infertility. What I do know is that there is hope for a life after this chapter. How blessed we are to be children of God! I rest in the assurance that I am loved and all of my sins are forgiven. Christ died for us all. Let us rejoice! Let us live!

I was born into, as well as married into, an incredible family that has a faith so deeply rooted that you cannot help but feel a stronger connection with the Lord each time you interact with them. I encourage you to find people like this to fill your life! Beautiful people with hearts so full for Christ with the understanding that we are so loved, even through sin. I admire both my parents and Ragland's parents for their steadfast love for our Father. I pray that Ragland and I continue to grow in our own faith, as individuals and as a couple. Through each obstacle we face in life, my prayers include "Let Your will be done."

## CHAPTER 16
# DON'T FORGET TO LIVE

During my final chemotherapy treatment, I sat in the hospital bed, twenty-four pounds lighter, tired, excited, and sad. I was leaving a place that I had called home for the past few months. I was comfortable there and knew that while I was attached to that IV pole with the handful of IV drips going into my veins, I would be safe from cancer. Even though my numbers had fortunately dropped drastically between the third and fourth treatment, I was still wary.

Was the chemo really doing its job? Were the doctors reading the numbers right? What if the cancer comes back? All of these questions and many more were filling my thoughts and making me forget about all of the progress I had made the past few months. I was almost in the clear. But I still could not see past the distracting thoughts and worries. My past nurses on the hall came into my room to count down the last seconds of the final chemotherapy drip. When the alarm went off to signal the bag empty, everyone in the room cheered, and many tears were shed. I looked around the room at all of these wonderful angels who had helped me beat this cancer, and I did not want to leave. I wanted to stay on that hall, where I knew I was safe. One of my favorite nurses, Lynne, could read it on my face. I was not going anywhere.

In that moment, she walked over and sat on the edge of my bed. She wrapped me in her arms and whispered in my ear, "Don't forget to live."

CPSIA information can be obtained
at www.ICGtesting.com
Printed in the USA
BVHW042143200520
580058BV00012B/378

9 781641 117463